Tears

Finding Purpose in The Pain

Dr. Michael Williamson

Tears: Finding Purpose in The Pain

Copyright © 2025 by Dr. Michael Williamson

Dr. Michael Williamson
michael.williamson@usd21.org

SoldOut Press International
Executive Editor – Chris Adams
Associate Editor – Dr. Jen Watkins

ISBN: 9798296900364

Dedication

"At twelve years old, I did it, confused, when my father told me he wasn't my father. At fourteen, I did it, scared, when my mother left me in an abandoned building. At sixteen, I did it, tired, when I slaved away washing dishes until midnight and supporting three kids while in high school. And at eighteen, I did it, broke, as I entered college. I'm still doing it."

~Author

Table of Contents

Foreword

This book is dedicated to the greatest hero in my life –
My mother, Patricia Minner.

My mother shed endless tears in silence, sadness, and
occasionally strength. She taught me more with her
vulnerability than words ever could. I learned empathy for
the forgotten, compassion for the broken, and understanding
for the abused. Above all, without opening the Bible, she
taught me the greatest lesson of all, forgiveness. Her life was
a sermon, and her tears wrote life-changing lessons on my
heart.

Patricia Minner.

The Teacher Who Changed the Equation

There was once a boy – angry, abandoned, and labeled "a
lost cause." The challenge of his upbringing began with the
death of his father when he was five. His mother remarried
and transferred all her love for her son to her new husband,
casting him aside to live with his grandparents. Raised by
grandparents, he carried wounds deeper than any report card
could measure. Every teacher called him "lazy…
unteachable… good-for-nothing." Then came his high
school head teacher, Henry Stokes, a devout Christian who
did not see the world as others did. He saw a pupil with

potential, a diamond in the rough. He spoke life into the young man. He believed when no one else would. That boy would go on to enthral the nations as none other than Sir Isaac Newton. Moreover, while the world remembers his laws of motion, heaven remembers the teacher whose faith-based inspiration set his young protégé in motion. Henry Stokes became the teacher who changed the equation.

God put a Henry Stokes in my life, too. His name was Mr. Doug Irons – my sixth-grade teacher. He was a coach, mentor, and an incredible father figure. In a society obsessed with race-based comparatives, division, and labels, his actions wrote a different narrative: a white man who believed in a Black boy others might have ignored. This counter-narrative to a severely polarized culture can help us see that good people are simply God's people. He did not just teach me a litany of meaningless facts–he taught me what every Father should teach his child: character. He did not just shape minds – he shaped destiny. I am no Newton in math, but I am Michael Williamson, a man with an unwavering desire to see the world evangelized. Moreover, like Newton, my tears became my testimony because someone believed I was more than my pain.

Hebrews 5:8 says, *"Though He was a son, He learned obedience from what He suffered."* That verse is not just about Jesus – it is about all of us who choose to be shaped rather than shattered by suffering. Pain taught me discipline. Abandonment taught me empathy for other people. Rejection taught me how to accept others and to be fiercely loyal. The world could not break me because the world did not make me. I was created in God's image.

Romans 8:28 reminds us, *"And we know that in all things God works for the good of those who love Him, who have been called according to His purpose."* God never wastes a hurt; He repurposes it for His glory. And **Isaiah 30:20-21** gives this promise: *"Although the Lord gives you the bread of adversity and the water of affliction, your teachers will be hidden no more; with your own eyes, you will see them. Whether you turn to the right or to the left, your ears will hear a voice behind you, saying, 'This is the way; walk in it.'"*

Mr. Irons was that voice in my wilderness. He did not just correct my behavior – he confirmed my worth. His belief in me became a prophecy I was determined to fulfill.

So, no, I'm not Isaac Newton; I'm Michael Williamson. However, like Newton, I am the product of a teacher who refused to overlook his students. Like Christ, I learned obedience through what I suffered. Moreover, today, I teach others how to rise from their own pain – because one teacher can always change the equation.

Foreword

Introduction

You have fed them with the bread of tears; you have made them drink tears by the bowlful. **(Psalm 80:5)**

I cried out to God for help; I cried out to God to hear me. When I was in distress, I sought the Lord; at night I stretched out untiring hands, and I would not be comforted. **(Psalm 77:1-2)**

As a homeless, fourteen-year-old, abandoned by a drug-addicted mother, my tears were my best friends. They were close companions, present through every sorrow, failure, and moment of confusion. God was feeding me with the *"bread of tears"* day and night. As the Psalmist said above, I sought the Lord in my distress.

If you are reading this book, you have suffered on some level and perhaps are still searching for the purpose within your pain. Trauma and pain are defined by emotional responses to past events that still affect individuals today. Prayerfully, you picked up this book because you want to do something vitally important; you want to strengthen your relationship with God through change. More specifically, you want to change your mind about suffering and pain. If change is not your motive or goal in reading this book, I encourage you to stop now until you are truly ready to be different. You will cry. You need to cry. Those tears may hold the key to healing from years of hidden trauma. Change can be painful, but nothing is as painful as being stuck in a place you do not belong.

This book is about taking control of the reverberating voice of injury so that it does not convert you into a "sold-out" victim of injury. There is no virtue in victimization. Many people have allowed their past injuries to take up residence in their minds, much like a bad tenant who refuses to leave. However, you do not have to be mastered by abuse, suffering, or trauma. With Jesus, you can seize control of every evil thought and force it to submit to Christ. **(2 Corinthians 10:5)** The Greek term *aichmalōtizō* (αἰχμαλωτίζω) translates literally to "to capture or lead away," which describes the action of seizing prisoners during wartime. It expresses the concept of using a spear to hold someone as prisoner and shows that thoughts can be made to obey our will, captured in the same way that prisoners of war are. Thoughts do not have to hold us captive.

Some thoughts belong inside our minds: truth, love, faith, purity, wisdom, confidence. Others are enemies: unholy fear, lust, irrational skepticism, bitterness. The Holy Spirit has given you the authority to stand guard – to block the intrusive thoughts, to fight aggressively if necessary, and to refuse to negotiate with them.

Picture yourself outside Buckingham Palace in London, which serves as the residence of one of the world's most influential monarchs. A guard completely clad in armor stands before you with a rifle and maintains steady eye contact as you advance. His presence alone declares: *You will not enter unauthorized. Any potential threat will be swiftly neutralized.* The palace is under 24-hour surveillance – no intruder slips in unnoticed. Now, apply this to the mindset of a true disciple. Satan, the accuser of our brothers, relentlessly tries to gain access to your mind. However, just as at Buckingham Palace, you are the guard – the gatekeeper – the hard-fighting soldier.

The enemy cannot walk into a fortified palace, but he can enter through an unguarded door. If you leave your mind unprotected, thoughts that should have been rejected at the gate will slip inside and take up residence – rent-free. This is why you must study the Bible. When the truth of God's word saturates your mind, you take every thought captive – you rule your mind instead of your mind ruling you.

While we possess the ability to refuse to let godless, intrusive thoughts dictate the narrative of our belief system, there are moments when we need to step aside, allow ourselves to be human, and fully feel the pain. The journey is not about merely hard work but the far more challenging "heart work." It is about allowing yourself to feel deeply, to let those tears flow, and to discover that through them, God may be preparing you for a profound transformation to draw you closer to him. This book will guide you in that process so that you can take the time you need to weep and then return to the battle and become the true master of your emotions.

It is comforting to know that God has led so many biblical characters through similar journeys. The Bible's first recorded account of tears does not belong to a rebel, a victim, or a hurting mother – it belongs to the father of our faith, Abraham. According to **Genesis 23:2**: *"Sarah died at Kiriath Arba (that is, Hebron) in the land of Canaan, and Abraham went to mourn for Sarah and to weep for her."* The Hebrew term for weep here is *Bakah* – "to shed tears in sincere grief." This was not a passing emotion. This was a soul-deep wail from a man who had walked with God and with this woman for decades of discipleship. Sarah had been Abraham's partner in the gospel through barrenness, bitterness, breakthrough, and belief. She laughed, she doubted, she hoped, and finally, she trusted. **(Hebrews 11:11)** Her death signalled the end of a covenant friendship, and Abraham did what every devoted disciple will ultimately have to do some day: he trusted God while he shed tears.

Tears are not a weakness but a way for faithful disciples to bear witness. They also humanize the greatest of heroes. Remember, Abraham lost his father along his way to Canaan, lost his wife, and at one point was called to sacrifice his son. David was also familiar with tears. **Psalm 56:8 (NLT)** states:

You keep track of all my sorrows.
You have collected all my tears in your bottle.
You have recorded each one in your book.

As David wandered the land, evading the relentless pursuit of either Saul, his son Absalom, or the Philistines, he poignantly captured the assurance that God meticulously accounted for every tear he shed in the psalms he wrote. Indeed, the comfort David expressed in **Psalm 56** serves as a reminder for us all. Knowing that God is aware of our pain and suffering helps tremendously in tough times. David found peace in realizing God counted every tear he cried. We also can trust that our struggles do not go unnoticed (not even the smallest).

Interestingly, ancient Greek and Roman cultures practiced collecting tears in small vessels known as lacrymatories, a tangible acknowledgement of grief and loss. These delicate little containers, often made of glass or pottery, served as tangible signs of grief and severe trauma. They preserved mourners' tears as physical manifestations of their grief and deep emotional distress. They did not hide their grief but acknowledged it as a part of life. **Psalm 56** indicates God doing the same.

In our modern world, however, our lacrymatories are not made of glass or clay; they are the human hearts that hold our pain. Just as those ancient vessels were a testament to the mourner's grief, our hearts and in some cases the physical human body stores the weight of our own sorrows. The ancient Greek author Aeschylus, called the "Father of Tragedy," wrote about the pain that remains unforgettable as it steadily impacts the heart. Our understanding develops from sorrow because of the wisdom carved into our being by every tear. Divine blessings frequently arrive after God has taken us through breaking moments. I believe God can help you heal as well, mending the cracks in your heart and turning your tears into a source of renewed strength and compassion.

I vividly recall wandering the streets of Portland, Oregon and Vancouver, Washington desperately seeking refuge from the uncertainty and fear that gripped my heart like a vice. I now realize that I was facing what you could easily describe as my darkest hour – like the one Britain faced in the beginning of World War II when they stood alone against Adolf Hitler's Nazi forces. Satan was launching a full-scale attack against my family, my faith, and my destiny, as **John 10:10** states: *"The thief comes only to steal and kill and destroy; I have come that they may have life…"* I remember the time that the thought of ending up in a nearby foster home sent chills down my spine because of stories of abuse and neglect circulating through the neighborhood. I vividly remember one kid who, shockingly, boasted that the abuse was not so bad, as if he had somehow come to accept, even enjoy, what was happening to him. The idea that someone could become so twisted by their circumstances terrified me. From an early age I was determined to be different. I was homeless, and more afraid than I had ever been in my life, and at the same time oddly persuaded that God would watch over me.

Amidst all the chaos and uncertainty in my own life, God was there. When I was a homeless fourteen-year-old student, hiding my tears from anyone who dared look into my eyes, God stayed right there. His presence was always strong – a constant comfort and strength. It did not matter how bad the storm got; He never forgot me. His love has carried me through everything, telling me I am seen, cherished, and always held in His embrace. The Lord watches over me, and the Lord watches over you.

As a young disciple, the moment I encountered **Genesis 50:20** was life changing. It was as if time had come to a standstill, and I momentarily transcended my physical existence, like the character Sam Wheat, played by Patrick Swayze in the movie Ghost, did. I could observe my own life and witness the profound healing power of redemption encapsulated in Joseph's words: *"Don't be afraid. Am I in the place of God? You intended to harm me, but God intended it for good to accomplish what is now being done, the saving of many lives."* **(Genesis 50:19-20)** Joseph's words are more than a declaration of forgiveness – they are a revelation of purpose. Through his tears, Joseph saw God's hand at work, even in betrayal and suffering.

This story unlocked something beautiful inside of me. Tears flowed down my face while bitterness dissolved my long-held rage which allowed me to recognize that this moment marked the beginning of my transformative healing journey to find purpose in my pain. I had been misunderstood, discarded as waste, and abandoned, but Joseph's perspective illuminated the purpose behind my struggles, revealing that what had been intended to break me was making me into a conduit for the greater good.

Later, as I grew as a disciple, I stumbled upon another profound nugget encapsulated in the timeless promise of **Romans 8:28**: *"And we know that in all things God works for the good of those who love Him."* This Scripture promised that nothing happens "to you" but "for you." Paul the apostle teaches us that every tear shed, every trial endured, and every pain experienced serves a greater purpose for those who love God. In my hardships, God was sculpting my spirit.

Perhaps, through these pages, He will start chiseling away at yours.

The alternative is unpleasant. As a Bible counsellor, I have guided numerous individuals through their emotional landscapes by focusing on healthy ways to address their anger – a typical byproduct of unaddressed trauma. Some, like the British, see tears as a form of embarrassment and adopt the "stiff upper lip" of unnatural emotional restraint and Stoicism. The national slogan from World War II in England was "Keep Calm and Carry On." This represented strength but encouraged people to suppress their grief and fear. The practice of emotional repression blocks people from presenting their struggles to God who invites us to share our burdens with Him because of his care for us. **(1 Peter 5:7)**

Yet modern thinking has led many to doubt God's benevolence. Many, like Rabbi Harold Kushner, ask the question, "Why do bad things happen to good people?" Throughout history people have continuously explored the reason why suffering exists. When Rome fell to the Visigoths in 410 AD, Augustine of Hippo stood in the ashes of an empire on the brink of collapse, declaring a timeless truth:

There is a City of God, and there are cities of men – and no matter how great the latter, they will fall.

Hindus use the concept of "*Karma*" or what Western philosophy defines as "What goes around comes around," teaching that present suffering stems from wrongful actions performed in past lives, while enduring present pain promises freedom from suffering in future lives. In the process they create a sense of callousness towards pain as something that is deserved. Buddhism asserts that suffering (or *dukkha*) arises from human desires (*Tanah*), advocating that relinquishing all desires eliminates the possibility of disappointment. Humanism places human beings at the center of the universe, asserting that happiness is self-created, and that God cannot truly help. In Richard Dawkins' atheistic view, suffering occurs because the universe is indifferent to human existence, lacking any inherent design or purpose and existing without any moral distinctions like good or evil.

These diverse answers to the problem of pain all have one thing in common: they are human solutions seeking to reconcile suffering without the involvement of God. In the 21st century, even those who believe in God, like Job's friends did in ancient times, can misunderstand the purpose of pain, associating prosperity with divine blessing and suffering with divine punishment. Yet the biblical narrative of Job demonstrates that a godly man can face tremendous suffering. Jesus experienced immense suffering without sin and showed that suffering does not necessarily stem from personal misconduct. Even though **Romans 3:10** states that no one stands as righteous before God, the Bible also teaches that suffering is not always a direct consequence of one's sin. **(John 9:1-3)** The common thread is that pain is an inherent part of every human journey, but the amazing assurance for Christians is that God is ever-present during their suffering. **(Hebrews 4:15)**

C.S. Lewis aptly characterizes pain as God's megaphone, amplifying His voice when nothing else can rouse a deaf world. Pain is a powerful means of communication for the physical human body, alerting us to threats or imbalances. A speck of dirt in the eye can cause excruciating pain but lie undetected elsewhere. When organs like your heart detect threats but lack receptors to pain, they borrow others' pain cells ("referred pain") which is why heart attack victims often report pain in the shoulder or arm. Pain is the most influential language the body can use to draw attention to something important.

God's painkiller is to cry. **Lamentations 2:19** states: *"Pour out your heart like water in the presence of the Lord."* Through their role as a physical and emotional release, tears act as a natural conduit to recovery. During emotional distress, human tears help remove dangerous stress hormones which otherwise can cause serious health problems not seen by the human eye; they flush out bodily toxins and boost immunity. They decrease manganese levels in the body, which otherwise would lead to anxiety or aggressive behavior or irritability. They also help the brain have a chemical reset, activating the parasympathetic nervous system to help you avoid numbing out or having a major outburst from built-up stress.

Pain exists not just to cause suffering but to enable personal growth and spiritual transformation through healing and deeper communion with God. Through accepting tears as powerful tools and understanding God's sovereign purpose in our suffering, we discover healing and hope throughout our life's challenges. Tears communicate, "I'm hurt," while simultaneously showing that your soul is undergoing healing.

Time, God's incredible chisel, acts as both a healer and a revealer. What may appear ugly or intolerable to you might be seen as beautiful from God's perspective. His viewpoint is eternal, and His timing is flawless. As **Ecclesiastes 3:11** states, *"He has made everything beautiful in its time."* If your circumstances haven't yet reached this state of beauty, hold on. The story isn't over. The anguish, heartache, and challenges you face are not without purpose – your suffering is the raw material for something breathtakingly beautiful.

This book aims to guide you toward accepting your tears as a sacred gift that reveals God's redemptive plan in your life. It is through moments of sadness and joy that our story finds depth, resilience, and character, allowing the hand of God to make what's broken beautiful. Let your tears become a sacred path to deeper intimacy with the God who holds you securely in His hand throughout all suffering. Rest assured that during your tears, God's eternal Word speaks words of comfort, assurance, and endless hope, and on that great final day, *"He will wipe away every tear from their eyes."* **(Revelation 21:4)**

Chapter 1: Tears of Brokenness

"Immediately a rooster crowed. Then Peter remembered the word Jesus had spoken: 'Before the rooster crows, you will disown me three times.' And he went outside and wept bitterly." **(Matthew 26:74b-75)**

Sometimes, when I'm alone
I Cry,
Cause I am on my own.
The tears I cry are bitter and warm.
They flow with life but take no form
I Cry because my heart is torn.
I find it difficult to carry on.
If I had an ear to confiding,
I would cry among my treasured friend,
But who do you know that stops that long,
To help another carry on.
The world moves fast, and it would rather pass by.
Then to stop and see what makes one cry,
So painful and sad.
And sometimes…
I Cry
and no one cares about why.

~Tupac Shakur

Chapter 1: Tears of Brokenness

Peter's denial of Jesus during the narrative of the cross can be described as an "epic failure, the classic unexpected defeat of one of the story's greatest heroes. Peter, the oldest of the disciples, is often portrayed as impulsive in speech to the point of trying to lead his leader. **(Matthew 16:22-23)** These accounts reveal that despite moments characterized by mistakes, Peter usually found his way back through mild correction or a gentle nudge by the Holy Spirit. Yet during the events surrounding Jesus's crucifixion, he comes to a pivotal crossroads in his life, where his arrogance is results in a humbling downfall through his denial of Jesus. He stands at a critical moment in his walk with God – his failure marked by the shedding of bitter tears.

Peter's personality is complex, oscillating between overconfidence, emotional instability, and shaky faith. Despite his previous passionate proclamations of fidelity, **(Matthew 26:31-35)** when confronted by adversity he gave in to a tidal wave of fear and desire for self-preservation. He did not "chicken out" in front of an angry Roman temple guard or steel-faced centurion! He buckled in front of a slave girl. Three denials and one rooster later, we have a tearful man aware of his own faithlessness. Yet these tears were his turning point, the very birthing waters of a new calling! If this can happen to Peter, and happen for me, then it can happen for you.

The lessons drawn from Peter's narrative are extensive. His inclination towards self-reliance and his hesitation to embrace humility provide a significant warning to true disciples. It is a poignant episode that starkly contrasts Jesus washing His disciples' feet – a task that Peter initially rebuffs, highlighting his reluctance to accept servitude over greatness.

Interestingly, Jesus admonished Peter to deny himself before predicting he would deny Jesus. This draws attention to the essential dilemma: succumb to self-rule or surrender to the liberating embrace of following the Word of God. Peter's story exemplifies this battle, culminating in a profound decision to let go of the ego. One could say ego stands for:

Edging
God
Out

Undoubtedly, each morning after the cross served as a relentless reminder of Peter's vulnerability; his disloyalty to his Master was painfully echoed in the rooster's call. The tears Peter shed, laden with sorrow and remorse, marked a pivotal moment of self-awareness and humility. It is in his brokenness that Peter finally faced the magnitude of his shortcomings – a vital step towards genuine transformation. Peter's denial of Jesus and his tears represent failure, redemption, and growth. From brokenness to restoration, his story provides hope and guidance for those navigating faith and personal transformation. His life also powerfully illustrates God's redemptive might. Only stripped of his ego could he emerge as a conduit for courage and conviction – a clear embodiment of grace's transformative capacity.

Chapter 1: Tears of Brokenness

On a sunny, unsuspecting afternoon in Lloyd Center Shopping Mall in Portland, Oregon, I was approached and evangelized by an unlikely figure – an actor. As I have spent part of my professional life as an actor, I can see God's sense of humor in this interaction. This encounter was profound, especially since I had recently received a Drammy Award[1] for my role in a stage play entitled, "The Treatment" by Martin Kremp. The director had praised my performance, suggesting I had a promising career in film and TV if I chose to move to Los Angeles, California. This revelation filled me with hope, a beacon in my quest for a purpose in life.

However, as I contemplated the move to LA, a persistent voice inside me strongly resisted. I had seen many actors from Portland move to LA only to return with deep drug and alcohol issues. Whether I was consciously aware of it or not, the mere thought of drugs was deeply unsettling to me. Growing up, I had received ample education about the dangers of narcotics, witnessing the devastating effects as one family member after another succumbed to their grasp, fading into a shell of their former selves. Despite being surrounded by all kinds of reckless sin, I had somehow avoided that form, understanding that the same fate could come to me if I were not careful.

That little voice also cautioned against repeating my mother's mistake – abandoning my daughter. This internal conflict tormented me for weeks until Dexter, that LA actor visiting Portland, invited me to church. His invitation felt like a divine intervention, an echo in the pit of my soul,

---

[1] Drammy Awards are awarded to talented actors in Portland, OR.

disrupting my Hollywood dreams and redirecting my thoughts towards God. Even at the swanky bar I was at later that evening, I could not enjoy the festivities, haunted by the invitation. I could no longer sin in peace. Later that night, I drove to a secluded park at 2am and wept bitterly, subconsciously realizing that God was calling me to give up the "act."

My first visit to church was unforgettable. The unity and power of the congregation singing together struck me more than anything else. Despite my attempts to mask my insecurity with a well-tailored Armani suit, I was too self-conscious, proud, and embarrassed to join in the singing. It felt like a huge neon spotlight was on me, highlighting my refusal to participate. I myself wondered why I was so nervous, given my frequent auditions in front of hundreds. However, this light was a different light than the one in theaters; it was the light of God that meant I was completely seen. By the final verse of "Rise Up, O Men of God," I found myself standing and singing with a conviction I had never experienced, breaking a belief instilled in me from my childhood that only exceptionally talented people should sing passionately.

The post-service Bible study was filled with personal questions that pierced through my façade of fear and deceit. Questions about my unnamed father, family upbringing, and life in general induced a nervous sweat, revealing how vulnerable and exposed I felt in this unfamiliar environment. This was a stark contrast to the confidence I wielded in auditions.

Chapter 1: Tears of Brokenness

Leaving the church, I felt relieved, yet unsettled, by the honesty and openness I had encountered. It was a challenge I was not ready to face. God, however, in His patience, had other plans for Michael Williamson. Over the next year I was invited to church by at least thirty different disciples, each invitation chipping away my resistance and drawing me closer to Jesus and His call for my life.

One particular disciple who seemed like an angel to me was Paul Williams. Paul persistently called me, so much so that I once returned his call only to point out that he had been trying to reach me for over a year. I was also called by the lead pastor a few times, but after I swore at him on the phone, he gave up. Paul's response, delivered in a voice so calm it disarmed me, was that he sought nothing more than to offer spiritual encouragement. Skeptically, I asked what he wanted in return. To my surprise, he suggested that we meet for lunch, leaving the choice of venue entirely up to me.

Living a life fueled by selfishness, arrogance, wild Vegas nights, and money, I was blind to acts of genuine kindness and humility towards others. So I chose the most expensive and trendy café in town, the Cadillac Café, a favorite among the Portland Trail Blazers[2] at the time. I casually scrutinized Paul throughout the meal, searching his face for hidden motives. My mind was a whirlwind of suspicion: Was he hiding his true sexual orientation? Was his generosity a mask for loneliness, compelling him to buy an expensive lunch for a stranger?

---

[2] Portland's professional men's basketball team.

Despite my doubts, our conversation was light, sprinkled with a few scripture references that were casual but convicting. Before I knew it, Paul was concluding our meeting, hurriedly leaving for work. This was a move I thought I would make, but it was almost as if Paul was one step ahead of me the entire time. To my shock, the deceitful twist I was waiting in suspense for the whole meal never materialized. I prided myself in the ability to spot the angles in any one-on-one conversation, but this time I was baffled. As he dropped me off and expressed a wish to keep in touch, he mentioned seeing leadership potential in me and envisioned me doing great things for God someday.

Watching his car disappear, a thought struck me – I had never experienced such unconditional love. In my world, unconditional love was as foreign as a tea party in the tower of Babel. Back in the solitude of my well-groomed, one-bedroom apartment, I sat on my futon sofa, overwhelmed by emotion. I reached up to sooth the itch on my face, only to realize I was crying. Tears slowly flowed as I realized God's kindness was gradually melting away the layers of skepticism and sin that had hardened my heart for years.

Usually, whenever emotions pushed me to the brink of tears, I would quickly wipe my face, masking my vulnerability behind a shroud of fear and embarrassment. Yet, in this moment, I found myself surrendering the cascade of tears, embracing their release without restraint. God was working on me.

Chapter 1: Tears of Brokenness

After every seriously humbling event in my life, I quietly made my way back to church without really talking about why I had returned. Each time I left a Bible study, I found myself in a twisted cycle – becoming even more sinful. I contracted an STD from one woman, passed it to another, and then lied to the hospital to get a second dose of medication. I did not want to tell the woman I had infected that it was chlamydia, so I told her it was just a urinary tract infection. I said the doctor had prescribed medication for both of us. She was humble and trusting, but the medication caused serious complications, driving the wedge of guilt even deeper into my heart.

I knew it was only a matter of time before I caught something pills could not fix. Yet, I did the same thing again. Once again, I decided I needed to go back to church, but my repentance was not real repentance. I call it crisis repentance.

During that time, I had several warning signs from God: speeding tickets, parking tickets, close calls with getting caught stealing from my company, increased visits to an adult bookstore I frequented. I even got into a fistfight inside a seedy adult bookstore, fighting off advances from gay men.

I had lied to so many people that there were days I would not even leave my apartment, paralyzed by the fear of being exposed in my own duplicity. However, one of the saddest, most soul-crushing moments of my life came when I left the home of a married woman. As I stepped out of her bedroom, her young daughter appeared in the hallway, expecting to see her father. Instead, she saw me. Her eyes welled with tears, and without a word, she turned and disappeared back into her room.

After that encounter, I sat in my car and wept. The weight of my choices crushed me because I had seen this before. I had lived this before. I remembered a similar moment from my own childhood – a painful memory of my mother's infidelity and the strange man I had accidentally run into. My godlessness was out of control.

There were also the near-death experiences: drunken nights out with friends that ended in gun violence. One night was so bad that a local drug gang shot up the club I was in – for the third time. One of those nights was terrifying. I was hiding behind a tire outside the club when the shooting started. A high-pitched whistle pierced the air – a bullet hitting the tire I crouched behind. I had almost been shot in the head.

I vowed to change after each of these near-death experiences, but once again, my repentance did not come from a true love for God – it was out of fear of being caught. This crisis repentance became my normal. Somehow, I thought a few Bible studies would help me slow down my reckless hedonism, but they did not.

Still, when the church reached out to me, I accepted their call to change. I had faced several humbling moments after leaving the church the last time, but maybe, just maybe, this time something they said would finally help.

"So, Michael, this marks the third time you've studied the Bible with us, each time delving into what it truly means to count the cost. We know your recent breakup has profoundly affected you, so this is the perfect moment for you to change. But are you seriously committed this time? Do you truly desire to embrace the life of a sold-out disciple?"

"Yes," I replied with unwavering conviction.

"That's wonderful! Please bring your clothes for baptism this Sunday."

However, when Sunday arrived, I was nowhere to be found. For reasons I still cannot fully articulate, the thought of committing to discipleship ignited a fear more terrifying than any childhood nightmare. Crisis repentance was not truly moving my heart. Deep down, I knew becoming a disciple meant confronting the memory of family incest, grappling with abandonment, and my obsession with graphic pornography. The fear I had at that time mimicked the one Moses described to the Israelites in **Exodus 20:20** when he said not to fear God. Instead of the fear that would keep me from sinning, I had the "unholy fear" that paradoxically kept me sinning!

Despite this, I found myself drawn to the Bible. For months I poured over its pages, captivated by its wisdom, while simultaneously leading a life that could not have been more at odds with its teachings. My heart had grown so calloused that nights often saw me transitioning without hesitation from Bible study to the darkness of nightclubs, immersing myself in a godless lifestyle I knew I needed to leave. The irony was not lost on me, but my conscience was dulled, numbed by the routine of living two lives. I was deeply immersed in a spiritual battle without knowing it.

The disciples were relentless in their love and unwavering in their faith, walking into my chaos like seasoned angelic prosecuting attorneys. They came armed with analogies that pierced through my defenses, insights that exposed cracks in my hardened hart, and arguments so compelling that they left me speechless, which is hard to do! Still, I resisted. It was not that I did not believe – they made God's call so clear I could not deny it – but I mocked it, clinging to my pride, my independence, and my refusal to surrender. I was so well-schooled in the Bible after coming around the church for so long that I would lead Bible studies, challenging others to get baptized before taking the plunge myself. I remember the second part of **Isaiah 57:11b**: *"Is it not because I have long been silent that you do not fear me?"*

One turning point came as I confronted a tangible fear of contracting HIV from my reckless lifestyle, a fear amplified by a friend contracting herpes, and the chilling news that an individual named Michael was charged with an attempted murder for knowingly infecting women with AIDS. This Michael frequented the same nightclub I did, a revelation that slapped me with the full force of a divine warning. **(Acts 12:7)** The darkness enveloped me so much that I found myself in an affair with an actress who, I later discovered, practiced witchcraft. It was a shocking revelation that extended beyond her; all the actors involved in the production were occultists. My nonchalant attitude had blinded me to the spiritual battle raging around me, a struggle for my soul as intense as the contest over Moses's bones. Yet, I continued a gamble with my destiny, each night's end marked by the haunting echo of my broken garage door, a metaphorical descent into darkness. A quiet voice would whisper, "You're heading to hell if you don't change, Michael," echoing Paul's transformation story. I was at the climax of evil.

> *Now, if I do what I do not want to do, it is no longer I who do it, but it is sin living in me that does it. So I find this law at work: When I want to do good, evil is right there with me. For in my inner being I delight in God's law; but I see another law at work in the members of my body, waging war against the law of my mind and making me a prisoner of the law of sin at work within my members. What a wretched man I am! Who will rescue me from this body of death? Thanks be to God – through Jesus Christ our Lord!* **(Romans 7:20-25)**

"Young man, get down; I said, get down!" The police officer's voice rang out, her tone exuding a mix of authority and maternal frustration towards another misguided youth caught in a tangle of lies and deceit. Rather than scolding, she addressed me with the tone of a caring mother, "Hands behind your head, son. Don't make this harder than it needs to be. How long have you known Charles? What is someone like you doing involved with a known criminal?"

Immediately in my head I started reciting the barber shop jokes that would certainly spread through the neighborhood: "Michael got arrested by someone's mom, a lady who smelled like cookies."

"I don't know what you're talking about!" I protested. I tried sounding convincing, but the guilt in my heart made my voice crack. I knew I was caught, and I had messed up big time this time. The sun shone bright that day while curious eyes peeked from behind window curtains, drawn to the spectacle. Despite the dry chill of a Portland winter, sweat cascaded down my face as if it were the height of summer. A whirlwind of emotions overwhelmed me: shock, embarrassment, sadness, anger, and paralyzing fear. For the first time I felt a genuine fear of God.

The car ride to jail was a ten-minute journey that seemed to last for days. As the car made its way through the streets, the world outside seemed to move in slow motion. Oddly, my mind began to replay vivid flashes of childhood – those days I spent running through the neighborhood with my brothers, imbued with a sense of joy and unburdened freedom. Back then, I was looked up to as a leader and cherished as an essential part of our collective lives. Now, here I was, bound for jail. At that moment time seemed to pause, suspending me between the cherished past and grim reality of my present. I was a failure, caught red-handed in sin. My chest began to swell, emotions bubbling up within, whispering, "Just let it out, Michael. Cry."

Chapter 1: Tears of Brokenness

My entire life flashed in front of me. This was the last day I was required to make the final payment on the condominium I had bought. The rent-to-own home-buying scheme worked perfectly if you paid your home deposit within a specific timeframe. Failure to pay meant I would lose the property. Losing the condominium as an adult subtly haunted my subconscious, reviving the deep-seated pain of losing our family home in childhood. I also had an apartment I was renting on the other side of town. The rent for that location was also in arrears for no reason other than pure laziness. I had the money to pay; I just did not have the discipline, and it had finally caught up with me. The two women I was mutually dating showed up at the exact time I was being arrested; their physical altercation was another public spectacle. I lost my job that day and over $8500 in bonus checks that reverted to the company, given my termination. The judgement I once held over family members with criminal records dissolved, as I no longer possessed the moral high ground. In my mind I had lost it all. My eyes welled up, and no matter how hard I tried, I could not hold back the tears.

Every Bible study over the past 18 months flashed across my mind like movie scenes. Conversation with disciples I did not take seriously emerged as my brain started recalculating data: "God can humble the proud; it is dreadful to fall into the hands of the living God, bro. God is going to flat humble you, bro! Just be holy!" exclaimed one of the voices in my head. It is fascinating how quickly we remember scriptures, insights, warnings, and sermons when facing life-altering moments. You either choose to fear God on your own, or He puts the fear of God in you Himself.

Once inside the holding tank, en route to my prison cell, I nervously surveyed the landscape. One man had the notorious teardrop tattoos under one eye, an indication of how many people he had murdered. Another man was foaming at the mouth because his body could not handle the 24 hours he had been inside with no heroin. One younger man, much younger than me, looked deeply sad. The horror escalated as a man resorted to retrieving swallowed drugs from his fecal waste on the jailhouse floor, a scene of desperation and degradation. Two other criminals quickly jumped down off their bunks and began helping the man go through the excrement until they found the drugs. Somehow, they lit a small piece of a match until it made a blaze of fire with toilet paper. The smell of drugs, the warmth of the jail cell, human sweat, and everything else made me nauseous.

Overwhelmed by the fear of God's judgment, my mind sought refuge in the most unexpected sanctuaries: the re-runs of talk shows I had routinely watched. A peculiar vision transformed my dreams of being an actor into a haunting nightmare. I imagined myself as the subject of a dramatic reveal on one of these shows (Geraldo, Montel Williams, or Oprah), the plot twisting the fabric of my reality into a narrative I had never desired but now deserved.

With a flair for the dramatic, the host would announce to an eager audience: "Ladies and gentlemen, tonight we have an extraordinary guest. Wrongfully imprisoned for three decades, he has endured a fate no script could fully capture. But today, at 50, he steps back into the world a free man. Drum roll, please, and join me in welcoming Michael Williamson to the stage." This fantasy, born from fear and flicker of hope, played in a loop in my mind, blurring the lines between my dreams of the spotlight, and the stark reality of what happens when you reject God's purpose for your life. **(Luke 7:30)**

I was moved to another jail cell that night, and as soon as I walked in, a massive Jamaican man erupted into this fourth-quarter football-style roar: "Oh yes, we have another one with us!" His voice hit me in the chest like a shockwave. "You ready to go to war, my brother?" he continued. The reality was that I had walked into a jail cell in the middle of a race war fight. I thought things like this happened only in movies, but the turmoil was real. Guards quickly pulled out guns and calmed the disturbance, then placed me in the cell.

After roughly five hours sitting there, looking at a host of repeat offenders and criminals, I realized I was no different. It was evident to me that my sin had cost me everything. I had lost my livelihood, and more important, I myself was lost. I realized then that there were two costs to count when becoming a disciple. There was the cost of voluntarily giving up everything or the cost of God taking everything. I began to weep bitterly at how deep into the darkness I had sunk, crying myself to sleep for hours, understanding that above all what made matters worse was that I was not a disciple. I had sinfully delayed moments to change because I believed I would get more. I knew full well if I died, I would go straight to hell. It took six days of bitter weeping in prison before I started realizing that God was sovereign. God was breaking me because He was making me.

Then I had a moment of serendipity in the jail's dimly lit corridor. A janitor, pushing his broom across the cold floor, swept up a large clump of dust, and an object caught my eye – a discarded Bible. I picked it up and devoured the New Testament, reading it two or three times a day until **Matthew 6:33** resonated with my profoundly: *"But seek first His kingdom and His righteousness, and all these things will be given to you as well."* It was as if a switch had been flipped inside of me. With newfound resolve, I vowed to pursue Him with all my heart, regardless of the consequences.

Then the day of my sentencing came. Awakened at 4am, I was escorted to court; my case was scheduled for 10am. Approaching the stand to plead guilty, clad in the degrading orange jumpsuit and stupid plastic sandals, unshaven and weary, I was confronted with the faces of those who once looked up to me. My actor friends, ex-girlfriends, former bosses, and close friends filled the audience, their presence slicing through me sharper than any rebuke the judge could muster. One friend was close to becoming a police officer, and I can still see the disdain on his face.

Suddenly, the judge spoke up, his voice slicing through the air like a razor: "Williamson... weren't you the kid who played for that high school sports team?" His words hit me like a freight train, his eyes drilling into me with a mixture of recognition, disdain, and the kind of authority that made the air thick with tension. The room was so quiet I could have heard a rat walking on cotton. I could feel the weight of every second as if time had frozen.

I tried to peer over the crowd with my peripheral vision, but I could tell everyone was waiting to catch my eye. I stared at the judge, and I am sure he saw that both eyes were bulging with tears ready to be released.

Then, his decision came, swift and unexpected: "I'm going to let you go, but mark my words – if I see you here again, I won't hesitate to throw the book at you. Get out of here!"

Just like that, I was free. The weight that had been crushing me for what felt like eternity was suddenly released, and for the first time in a long time, I could breathe. It was the end of the old version of Michael – and the beginning of God doing something far greater.

Three weeks later, with tears of gratitude in my eyes and my head bowed low in shame and disgrace, I stood before a swelling crowd of 500 sold-out disciples. With every ounce of humility in my heart, I confessed Jesus as my Lord and Savior and was baptized in the back of a pickup truck in an ice-cold horse trough on January 23, 2000. It was minus five degrees that day, and for some reason I did not even feel the cold. Everything went in slow motion as they sang the words, "We love you with the love of the Lord." I had made it! I could not believe it, but I had. The weight of the world was gone, replaced with the unshakeable peace that only Christ could offer.

Matthew, Mark, and Luke provide a consistent account of Peter denying Jesus three times during His time before the Sanhedrin, and John's Gospel presents no conflicting details. Luke positions the denials before Jesus's trial by the Sanhedrin, **(Luke 22)** which contrasts with Matthew and Mark who place the denials afterwards. **(Matthew 26:57-75; Mark 14:52-72)** This understanding likely stems from Luke's mention of a trial at daybreak.

Matthew illustrates Peter's private courage yet public denial of Jesus as an extreme contradiction. After affirming Jesus as the Son of God, **(Matthew 16:13-19)** Peter remains silent during the trial and denies him three times. **(Matthew 26)** The account in Matthew reveals Peter's mounting desperation to distance himself from Jesus, using curses and oaths to try to fit in with the crowd while betraying his identity and his Lord.

The narrative also stands out by noting Peter's unique Galilean accent. **(Matthew 26)** This subtle yet revealing detail underscores the significance of Peter's effort to distance himself from Jesus. Researchers recognize the intricate dialectal distinctions within Aramaic that indicate Galilean Aramaic, which meant Jesus had the same accent as Peter. The inclusion of information about Peter's accent in a Gospel directed at Jewish audiences highlights his wavering faith, since he denied knowing Jesus despite linguistic similarities between them.

In the Gospel of Mark, a poignant detail emerges – the rooster crowing twice, once as Jesus predicted. **(Mark 14)**

The rooster crowing a second time confirmed Jesus's prediction. **(Mark 14:72)** Peter was ignoring God's grace expressed through clear warnings.

Luke's Gospel depicts Peter as he walks behind Jesus at a distance, representing his fears and self-deception before his eventual denial. The story encourages us to think about our tendency to inflate our dedication while bypassing the deep self-assessment required by biblical teachings. Peter's story serves as a powerful warning about how disloyalty can hide behind false commitment.

Luke's Gospel also captures a gut-wrenching detail unique among the accounts of Peter's denial. After Peter denied Him the third time, Jesus turned to look directly at Peter. Luke records Jesus performing a complete reversal through the verb *strapheis ho kurios,* which uses the second aorist passive participle form of *strepho.* Luke's exclusive description shows Jesus intentionally turning around to establish eye contact with Peter. The Greek word *emblepo* defines such a look because it represents both a glance and an intense examination. Jesus locked His eyes with Peter, who would later lead His church, and this moment delivered a message of realization and guilt that would torment Peter throughout his life.

This was the moment in which Peter felt a sword pierce his heart, experiencing our Lord's deep disappointment and searching gaze. Solomon explained that *"When a king sits on his throne to judge, he winnows out all evil with his eyes."* **(Proverbs 20:8)** Jesus's steady look either detected the disbelief within Peter's heart or served as a means to prompt repentance. The Chronicles also teach us that God's eyes roam the earth to reinforce those who dedicate their hearts completely to Him. **(2 Chronicles 16:9)** So we are left to ponder: was Jesus' look at Peter a rebuke or a strengthening encouragement?

The Luke account suggest that Jesus looked at Peter with eyes full of love and compassion when He turned to see him. The weight of Christ's compassion for Peter, who had received the name Peter (Greek for rock) and was expected to become a leading support of His mission, must have burdened him greatly. The devastation to Peter of his betrayal of Jesus was far greater because he stood before a Jesus who looked upon him and saw the betrayal directly. The harsh truth of our shortcomings becomes intolerable when we find ourselves spiritually trapped with our sins exposed before us.

The Gospels also enrich our understanding of Peter's response. The Greek term for "wept bitterly" in **Matthew 26:75** is *klah'-yo,* signifying a loud wailing born from deep, uncontainable grief. This vivid description paints a picture of Peter, overwhelmed by the magnitude of his betrayal and sin against the Lord, responding with uncontrollable weeping. Mark also highlights Peter's intense remorse through his depiction of Peter breaking down. The Greak language uses the term *epibalon,* which means "to throw oneself." Perhaps, like Jesus "throwing himself" to the ground in prayer earlier in the same chapter, **(Mark 14)** Peter cast himself to the ground while weeping bitterly. **(Mark**

14:35) The rooster's crow would become a haunting reminder of Peter's broken promise to God and undoubtedly kept him humble the rest of his life.

My own experience of shame and embarrassment from being imprisoned after my sin was revealed helps to keep me humble today. The truth about God's clear calling to serve Him and everything I learned in my Bible studies came back to me only once I fell into trouble. I was no different from Peter.

At 19 years old, Charles Haddon Spurgeon began his ministry at New Park Street Chapel, where he preached a powerful sermon based on **Mark 14:72**. At age 58, Spurgeon ended his ministry at the 6000-seat Metropolitan Tabernacle that he had supervised building. During his sermon, "Foundation of Repentant Tears," held on October 24, 1880, Spurgeon emphasized how brokenness leads to tears of true repentance. He articulated that genuine repentance entails profound godly sorrow for sin, not merely regret at being caught. Spurgeon effectively conveyed that true repentance, a divine blessing, is claimed only through tears:

> TRUE repentance is always the gift of God and the work of the Holy Spirit in the soul. Man, left to himself, continues in sin. If he turns from his iniquity, it is because God turns him. By nature, his mind is set on mischief, and if that mind is changed, as it is in genuine repentance, it must be because the Lord Himself has changed it. That repentance which a man works in himself, without the Spirit of God, will turn

out to be a repentance that needs to be repented of, but that godly sorrow for sin, which the Spirit of God produces in the heart, is a sure indication of spiritual life, and the constant attendant of saving faith. Whosoever unfeignedly repents of sin and believes in the Lord Jesus Christ is a saved man; he shall be among the blessed ones in that day when Christ comes to judge the quick and the dead; and he shall be among the glorified forever.

Yes, while repentance is wrought in men by the Spirit of God, He generally uses means to produce that result. In the case of Peter, the agency employed was thought – thought about his sin: "When he thought thereon, he wept." There is no doubt that multitudes of sinners have been led to repentance in this way; and, in some respects, this must be the universal way by which the Spirit of God conducts men to the goal of true penitence. As long as they live carelessly and thoughtlessly, they go on in their evil ways; but if they are stopped in their mad career, if they are made to consider if they begin to think over their sin, if God, the Holy Ghost, convinces them of the guilt of it, He uses that thought and conviction to lead them to trust in Jesus Christ. The remembrance of sin committed is the Holy Spirit's frequent if not constant method of bringing men to weep over their wrong-doing and to turn from it.

The day I emerged from the fleeting stint behind bars, I was ushered into a courtroom, not merely composed of wood and stone but one that seemed to judge the very essence of my being. I felt like a coward, confronted by my repeated failures to heed the path of righteousness and embrace the Bible as my standard. The eyes that met mine were filled with disdain and disappointment, reflecting a collective judgement that weighed heavily on my spirit.

I confronted my shortcomings in the presence of God and the people around me during a transformative day. This defining moment stands as one of the most humbling experiences in my life! I then moved to the arduous journey of intense self-discovery and true repentance. What started as a steady stream of hot tears and a profound longing for God ended with a transformation far beyond my wildest dreams.

Standing before a judge that day helped me understand that I was facing reality in the courtroom of life. A day would come when the judge would not be a fallible human but a living God. In that moment I realized that you are born looking like your parents, but you die looking like your decisions. Every decision I had made up to that point was set to ruin my destiny. The mercy I received at that point was my actual turning point!

The tears marked the start of the transformation I desperately needed. They served as an emotional release that manifested my soul's deep desire for change and for the essential role of God in my life. I felt a connection to Peter's path to repentance and renewal from **John 21:15-19** during that transformative moment. I was ready to move past my previous life and embrace a fresh beginning.

The opening of my heart taught me that my past life had been empty because it was controlled by pride and ego. I needed to start a true journey towards self-discovery, demanding humility and persistence while maintaining absolute faith in God's grace. I found renewed purpose in my spirit which now sought to become a conduit of God's glory while being shaped by His divine will.

Chapter 1: Tears of Brokenness

Chapter 2: Tears of Truth

"Truth is incontrovertible. Panic may resent it. Ignorance may deride it. Malice may distort it. But there it is."
~Winston Churchill

During the days of Jesus's life on earth, He offered up prayers and petitions with loud cries and tears to the one who could save Him from death, and He was heard because of His reverent submission. Although He was a son, He learned obedience from what He suffered and, once made perfect, He became the source of eternal salvation for all who obey Him and was designated by God to be high priest in the order of Melchizedek. **(Hebrews 5:7-9)**

The question of why we suffer is as old as humanity itself. The Epistle to the Hebrews serves as a spiritual text aimed at comforting Jesus's followers who struggled to understand pain during a challenging period in the history of Christianity. The writer of Hebrews sought to reaffirm to its original audience and modern readers that surviving these hardships served a meaningful purpose. The challenges faced by believers involved substantial losses, including their wages and property and sometimes their very lives. Facing hardships could lead true believers to abandon their faith, making the threat of apostasy a real possibility. The book of Hebrews addresses the early Christians' suffering by providing consolation along with an encouragement to remain steadfast.

Though addressing a specific historical context,[3] Hebrews transcends its time by speaking to a universal human experience of suffering. The early disciples were encouraged to see their trials not as meaningless or punitive but as part of a larger narrative in which faith is refined and strengthened. These teachings appear almost prophetic as they show us that our current struggles mirror the challenges faced by early disciples in a world increasingly unfriendly to Christians. Our current understanding of faith during times of hardship shows Jesus' important question continues to resonate through the ages: *"When the Son of Man comes, will He find faith on earth?"* **(Luke 18:8)**

The trials endured by the early Christians underline a broader, timeless inquiry into the purpose of pain and tears in changing the world with the Gospel. How does one stay committed in an uncommitted generation when subjected to overwhelming suffering? The answer is not in avoiding suffering, but in understanding and embracing trials as transformative processes that fortify faith, foster perseverance, and refine character. As we evangelize the world, we will face various trials – leadership apostasy, personal loss, societal injustices, or internal struggles with

---

[3] The book of Hebrews is believed to have been written at a point in the early church's time when disciples were being severely persecuted. There were two such periods. The first was around AD 64. Roman Empire senator-historian Publius Cornelius Tacitus reports that Emperor Nero enforced widespread persecution against Christians after the devastating fire in Rome on July 19. Nero wanted to shift suspicion that he started the fire so he accused the Christians. There was a second period of persecution in the first century during Domitian's reign from AD 81-96.

doubt. Hebrews invites us to look beyond the immediate pain and see the potential for growth, deepening our faith, and standing firm in the face of adversity.

The author of Hebrews presents several strong reasons for believers to seek meaning in their suffering. He points out that their struggles are for the One who remains constant across time – yesterday, today, and forever. **(Hebrews 13:8)** They do not endure hardship for a distant deity, but for a Messiah who intimately shares in their pain, unlike the gods of surrounding cultures. Every tear they shed is shared with God, who experiences their suffering alongside them. **(Hebrews 2:10-18; 12:1-11; cf. Acts 3:15; 5:30-31)** The book of Hebrews issues a powerful call to endure, as the writer likens the Christian journey to a race set before them. **(Hebrews 12:1)** Jesus Himself remained steadfast in His suffering. As His followers, we, too, should emulate His fortitude. **(Hebrews 12:3)**

Yet the Scripture quoted at the beginning of the chapter mentions that Jesus learned obedience through what He suffered. The question arises whether that happened because He had prior disobedience. We need to review **Hebrews 4** to gain the context. The author explains that because Jesus the Son of God has become our great high priest who ascended into heaven, we must maintain our confession of faith. Our high priest experiences our weaknesses because He faced every temptation like us but remained without sin. **(Hebrews 4:14-15)**

This establishes a key principle: Only faith which survives testing proves its genuine trustworthiness. Jesus had always had untested obedience. In heaven He had never experienced any temptations because all went according to God's will. It was only on earth, by experiencing and overcoming temptation, that He could move from untested obedience to tested obedience. It wasn't that He had ever been disobedient. It was that nothing had ever come across His path until He lived on earth to tempt Him to disobedience. Think of a healthy individual learning a new exercise like push-ups. Their excellent health enables them to perform the push-ups correctly each time. Even if they are unfamiliar with the technique, they ace every attempt. Similarly, Jesus faced many temptations to disobey God and aced every one. He could not "learn obedience" through suffering until He faced the real choice whether to obey or not. He overcame each challenge without fail, thus learning obedience from experience.

The Greek language used in **Hebrews 5:7-9** enhances our understanding. The term translated as "learn," *manthano*, signifies "to acquire knowledge and skill through instruction." Suffering allows us to acquire insight. Jesus attained understanding of our lives through righteous suffering, like David in **Psalm 22**. The Greek word for obedience, *hupakono*, means "to listen, respond, obey." Jesus acted under the Father's authority, attentively listening and submitting to His will. The text indicates that Jesus was made "perfect" (*teleios*), signifying "complete, mature." **Hebrews 2:10** supports this assertion: *"In bringing many sons and daughters to glory, it was fitting that God, for* *whom and through whom everything exists, should make the pioneers of their salvation perfect through what He suffered.*" Thus, Jesus was made "ready" for His role as Savior through suffering. In a similar way, our suffering enhances our spiritual growth.

The writer of Hebrews emphasizes that Jesus met His most significant challenge to His obedience – the cross – with prayer and tears. They contributed to Jesus's perfection, maturity, and completeness. This liberating truth reminds us that we need not strive for perfection in a self-reliant way because Jesus has already accomplished it. We follow a Savior who bore suffering for our sake. It also reminds us that often the way to our own maturity lies through suffering, prayer, and tears.

Suffering became such a constant in my life that I began to fear its absence. By the time I was three years old, I had already witnessed a man being hurled through a plate-glass window at the hands of the man I believed to be my father. Violence was not a guest but a permanent resident. It did not knock before entering; it lived on our doorstep breathing in the silence between my mother's screams.

At five, I was sent to live with my grandmother after my mother separated from the man I had always believed to be my father. Their relationship had been controversial from the start – my mother was a teenage girl of seventeen when she hooked up with this man who was more than twice her age. The elders in our family condemned the relationship, but their moral outrage was laced with hypocrisy. They all had a lot of sin buried in generations of religious, pharisaic silence. They preached virtue with trembling voices, but behind closed doors there was so much vile sin that their words felt like a performance.

After all, the family harbored a horrifying secret – one that haunted me even as a child. There was talk, whispered in hushed tones, that my mother had been raped by my grandfather while lying helpless in a hospital bed, eight months pregnant with me. Some even murmured that my uncle might have been my true father. No one dared speak these things aloud at family barbecues, but the weight of their silence was deafening.

To this day, I do not know whether my father was my grandfather, my uncle, or another nameless ghost in the dark corners of our family history. What I do know is that my mother carried her trauma like a wound that refused to close, and when she looked at me, she saw nothing but a living reminder of her pain. She cried a lot. Nothing makes a child sad like seeing their mother sad. That helpless feeling still makes me feel like I am losing air.

I lived with my grandmother while my mother tried to reclaim her teenage years that motherhood had stolen from her. She partied with reckless abandon, seeking escape in the arms of men and the haze of the 80s drug and party scene. However, the truth was inescapable. She had been beaten in my grandmother's home while carrying me in her womb, the blows landing with the cruel hope that they might force a miscarriage, erasing the evidence of possible family incest or shame.

By the time I turned seven, my mother had entered into another relationship, this time with a man twenty years her senior. His name was Billy. She was 23, a mother of three boys with another child on the way, and she was about to step into another world of pain that would become our normal. Shattered plates, overturned furniture, and the deafening roar of arguments were as familiar to us as the ticking of a clock. Billy's fits of rage would leave our home looking like a war zone, but I turned it into a game, pretending with my brothers that we were soldiers navigating a battlefield of debris.

When the police arrived – called by worried neighbors – my mother would pull herself together, smoothing her clothes and forcing a radiant, practiced Ebony magazine smile. "Everything is all right," she would tell them, her voice steady, her lies effortless. If they asked if they could speak to her privately, she would instantly fake an illness. I do not know how she did it, but the police always left, and when the doors were shut and the silence settled in, it was suffocating.

After Billy's drunken tirades, my mother would gather us close, her voice shaking as she prayed through her tears. Her voice would shake as she gave nervous kisses to us all on the tops of our heads. "You're my boys, I'm sorry," she would whisper, her fingers gripping our small hands. "I'm so sorry." And then she would sob, calling on God for mercy, for strength, for a way out. She had no idea that in those moments, she was teaching us to turn to the only One who could understand our suffering. **(Hebrews 4:15)**

Some nights I would escape to my older cousin's house, but relief never came. His girlfriend had a way of making my skin crawl. She would pull me aside and whisper, "You can keep secretes with me." I soon learned what those secrets were – drugs, alcohol, and hours of grotesque pornography plastered across a large screen, with several adults and young children between twelve and thirteen watching in a weird, guilty silence. She was quietly grooming us to do unspeakable things. I was only eleven or twelve at the time and she was twenty-two. I am sure she would have been arrested for abuse if someone reported her. There were children in our family who suffered unimaginable things at her hands, and to this day I do not know how I was spared but by the grace of God. However, the scars of what I saw remain.

Back home, the cycle never broke – only thickened like a stormy, Portland night. Billy's violence escalated, his addiction tightened its grip, and my mother fell deeper into a hole. When my brothers and I finally realized the full extent of his abuse of our mother, we decided: Billy had to die. We were just children, but hatred burned in us like fire. We plotted, whispering in the dark about ways to make it happen. My brothers were ready. Weapons were within reach.

The scary thing is we would have done it. There was an anger in the eyes of my brothers that let me know they were serious. Somehow, as the oldest brother, something inside me said, "Michael this is wrong, and you know it." If I had not been the voice of hesitation, of reason, perhaps we would have done it. I shudder to think what would have become of us then, possibly some twisted urban version of the Menedez brothers without the financial element.

We were surrounded by drug use. The pungent stench of crack cocaine, sweat, and burning plastic filled the air in certain rooms of our house, so thick it clung to our skin. It was itchy. Passive inhalation was unavoidable, and the sight of my mother – once just a smoker, now a full-blown crack addict – was unbearable. She lost a lot of weight, and I hated seeing her this way. Hunger felt like it chewed our stomachs to pieces constantly, and good food was a luxury we could not afford.

Sometimes we had to steal food from a grocery store called "Safeway." We had to choose survival over dignity and innocence as kids. Desperation led us to deception. At the time, an eerie voice in my head said, "Michael, this is not the 'Safeway.' This is not the 'Safe way' to survival. This is not the 'Safe way' to becoming a man." It was a far cry from the Safeway for hope. But it was the only way we made it through.

My mother obtained UNICEF donation boxes – the small cardboard containers covered with images of emaciated children, designed to stir the hearts of strangers. We went door to door, pleading for donations, but the money never went to charity. It bought our dinner instead. Some people were kind, pressing coins into our hands with tears in their eyes. It was clear that we were the UNICEF kids. Others were cruel, slamming doors in our faces. As the eldest, I understood the shame of it.

At school as a young kid I was bullied for my second-hand clothes, for my dark skin, for the simple fact of my existence in an all-white neighborhood. But nothing compared to the day that the man I had believed all these years to be my father, who through all these years I would visit on weekends with my younger brother, looked me in the eyes and told me the truth: "I am sorry, Michael. I am not your real father." Later, the words would play over and over in my head like a cruel, endless static on an old transistor radio. I sat alone at the kitchen table, my mother asleep in the next room, oblivious to the devastation unravelling inside her oldest son. This gave me the freedom and the opportunity to replay what I had just heard, no matter how brutally it was delivered.

"You are not a good child, Michael, and this is all happening because of you," I thought. Though I reminded myself that by this time I was a straight-A student, basketball team captain, and now popular at school, it did not help. Emotions overwhelmed me, and the dam suddenly burst like a flood. That day, consumed by sorrow, I did the only thing that made sense: I cried.

Every joke, every side-eyed glance at family gatherings suddenly made more sense. For the first time, I saw the truth staring back at me, and it swallowed me whole. Two years after my father informed me that he was no longer my father, things took a gradual turn for the worse. My mother and Billy began fighting a lot more frequently. But the disputes seemed more out of place, given the fact that my Billy had secured a high-paying job. We were also living in a better neighborhood, and I was attending an upper-middle-class school. Life seemed on the up and up. Although I did not know where Oxford or Cambridge was located, I was determined to attend these schools alongside my peers. Many of my school friends casually spoke of Ivy League schools like department stores. I spent time in their homes and saw a future I told myself I would have someday. For a moment, I dared to believe in a different life, I had a dream.

I was twelve when I first dreamed of a future beyond all this. My school friends would typically leave for the summer, so I would not see them until early fall. They spoke of international travel like a weekend ball game. Their homes were warm, their families whole. I clung to the hope that I could have that, too. I excelled in school, joined the honor roll, the debate team, varsity basketball.

Then my Garden of Gethsemane arrived. After separating from Billy, my mother disappeared on a three-month drug binge, leaving me, at fourteen, to care for my three younger brothers. I was a child, raising children. We survived on makeshift meals by eating cheese toast alongside the homemade bread I learned to make in school. I also developed a skill at using the barbecue in the backyard to cook virtually anything, and boiled water on the barbecue grill to make baths and wash our clothes. We stole water by night from the local church. We filled empty milk jugs with the water and hurried back to the house in hopes that no one saw what we were doing. The best time to steal the water was at night, but it was difficult to see the water tap so we chose early mornings. We then boiled the water on the barbecue grill, then poured it into a large square Coleman water cooler filled with laundry detergent to wash our clothes. The water cooler had extreme insulation, which created a steaming effect on the inside.

We turned every hardship into a game because reality was too crushing to bear. One time, before we began our normal jostling back and forth of the watercooler, I noticed the sad look on the face of one of my brothers, and I quickly scrambled for some story to justify what we were doing. "Don't cry, Perry; everything is fine, see." I purposely went somewhere in my mind to turn the tragedy of the moment into an emotional adventure for all of us. Maybe we were not washing our clothing with stolen water from a local church in a Coleman water cooler? Maybe it was some bad dream? Mom will be home soon, and we will not have to cry anymore, right? How did other homeless people wash their clothes on a day-to-day basis? So, we pretended we were on a roller coaster by rocking the water cooler back and forth. We were simulating a washing machine, and it worked like a charm. It stopped my brother from crying, and it stopped me from giving my heart emotionally to how depressing the situation was.

I lit candles at night to make sure I could see if my brothers were sad. We lived in perpetual fear, terrified that one day the state would come for us and take us away to a boys' home, a grim fate that was all too close to our shattered reality. The boys' home was a short distance from where we lived. Sadly, this place was filled with young boys who were being consistently sexually abused and raped. The neighborhood wasn't that big, so we knew some of the kids in the home.

After three long months, my mother returned–but not with the warmth of reunion. Without a word to me, she took my brothers away from school, leaving me to return to a home that was now painfully empty. She needed visible proof to continue receiving government assistance, and my brothers became her downpayment to the state – they were treated like currency for more money, more drugs. There was no EBT card in 1989. The system was different then – not stronger in support, but stronger in its power to reinforce shame, guilt, and the inescapable feeling that you were less than human. Public assistance programs like Aid to Families with Dependent Children (AFDC) didn't just provide aid; they demanded proof of desperation. Assistance wasn't just given; it was extracted through humiliation. But when you're smoking crack daily, you lose the ability to feel guilty.

I came home to an empty house – no food, water, light, or love. The lights, water, and electricity had been shut off six months ago, but with my brothers by my side, everything always felt just a little bit right. I was sadder seeing my brothers gone more than anything. It still hurts me deeply. I often cried myself to sleep by candlelight. Sometimes I was completely alone; sometimes the house, which was a wreck, was filled with several addicts who had a habit of drifting in and out.

I lived in that house alone for an entire year. One of the rooms was disgusting; it was filled with trash all the way to the ceiling, bulging at the door. If anyone saw the towering heap of trash piled up in front of our home, they would immediately know the house had long been abandoned. Thirteenth Street was no joke. The room itself was in ruins, having been transformed into a crack-smoking hideout for an entire year before. Every week, we had held our noses and tossed our garbage into the already claustrophobic bedroom until the mound grew so immense that the door could no longer be opened. At night, the sounds of scurrying, scratching rats, and rustling possums became a haunting rhythm, a constant reminder of my disgusting surroundings. The stench of decay and neglect was overwhelming, seeping into every corner of my existence.

Losing a mother was heartbreaking enough, but being separated from my brothers cut even deeper. Night after night, I lit candles in a desperate attempt to fend off the oppressive gloom, the flames reflecting the tears that streamed down my face as I cried myself to sleep. I could tell because sometimes I would look into the mirror. The whispers of the neighborhood were relentless – everyone knew the truth about the house I called home; it was a crack house. It had been one for a while. I was too terrified to acknowledge it, too afraid of the reality that I lived in a crack house for an entire year at fourteen years old, alone.

Some nights, terror gripped me as I realized that drug dealers roamed the place. Their presence was a constant threat because both doors were damaged and therefore unlocked. For an entire year, I endured the torment of living alone in that crumbling crack house, a silent witness to a life overshadowed by despair and isolation.

During the night, I would go outside and stare up at the stars, wondering if God heard my tears. These moments often found me standing alone in the backyard of the condemned home where I was staying. Subconsciously, I was compelled to pray, though I do not think I fully grasped the depth of my longing. The uncertainty of where I would go, the weight of abandonment – first at six years old with my mother, and now again – drove me to God in a way I did not even recognize at the time.

The pain was overwhelming, yet I had no idea that my actions were deeply connected to the training my mother had instilled in me. She had hurt me profoundly, but in her own way, she had also planted in me a subconscious reliance on God. Her internal struggles as her life spiraled out of control forced me to pay an unbearable price. I had to carry her burdens without a choice, but God's mercy granted me the resilience that became essential for my survival and strength base. The price I paid because of my mother's demons through loneliness, anger, and fear resulted in life-altering resilience.

My daily routine remained unchanged since I was still homeless and uncertain about what tomorrow would bring, but I managed to endure day after day without losing all hope.

William Shakespeare's *Macbeth*, Act 4 Scene 3, presents Macduff as he expresses despair over his country's suffering under Macbeth's oppressive rule: "Every new morning brings fresh cries from widows and orphans while fresh sorrows assault heaven to such an extent that it echoes Scotland's agony in mournful cries." (4.3.4–8) Macduff describes Scotland as a nation submerged in sorrow so powerful that the heavens themselves appear to weep with the nation's pain. While praying as a homeless teenager under the night sky, I clung to the hope that God would listen.

But the lies I told myself had become impenetrable. For years as an adult, I convinced myself that my childhood was not so bad, that everyone faced struggles like mine, that the past had no hold on me. It was not until the age of twenty-five that I finally acknowledged the dysfunction I had endured.

It is no surprise that this was also the year I was baptized.

My mother reappeared after a long, agonizing year, coincidentally, on the very day the police arrived to shut the house down. A year had already passed, and I was full of anger, resentment, and bitterness at the tender age of 14. My mother was totally oblivious to my pain. She even greeted me with a huge hug and a smile, as if things were okay. But as I looked outside, I saw my brothers in a car parked out front, with the driver clearly high on drugs.

That was when I finally told her what she had never been brave enough to say: "I am on my own now, Mom." It was liberation mixed with fear and insecurity in one. How do you mix freedom with pain in one moment?

"You're going to be okay, son," she replied quickly, as if those words could erase my loneliness and abandonment. How do you tell a 14-year-old boy that he is expected to survive independently? In that moment, I understood the truth – this was the power of Satan, tearing families apart and leaving a young soul to fend for itself. I stepped out onto the street, a surprising surge of confidence carrying me away from that forsaken house. It was liberating for a while, and in a weird twist, it felt right – the irony of the sunny, beautiful day clashing with the darkness that had defined my life was not lost on me.

For a while, hours slipped away in a futile distraction of video games at the corner store – the only escape a 14-year-old could find. The joystick became my friend, and enemy of my frustration all at once. Then the light faded, and a haunting darkness descended, leaving its scars on my heart. I came to the realization that I had nowhere to go. The daylight faded, and so did the illusion that video games would make it all go away. This was not a bad dream. This was reality. This was my life. Homeless at 14 years old, what would you do? Thank God I found refuge with a friend for a few days, a small haven of hope during my storm.

Jesus trains us by storm. **(Mark 4:35-41)** I realize now that the first miracle in life is not that the storm ended; it was that I survived. The second miracle is what I became as a result. I wasn't handed all the answers that day, but through it, God handed me perseverance. The tragedy of abandonment allowed suffering to become my teacher, not my tormentor.

I wasn't just surviving the streets; I was unknowingly learning how to shepherd souls, hear silent screams, and recognize pain behind pride. Years later, as a leader, husband, father, and a man of God, I can meet young men who wore the same scared look I once had. And I do not offer clichés – I provide compassion not because I was better, but because I remember. I remember the empty streets, the video game escapism, the silence after sunset. I remember how it felt to pray for someone to see me, and for no one to come. But now I know... He was there.

> Did you hear about the rose that grew
> from a crack in the concrete?
> Proving nature's law is wrong it
> learned to walk without having feet.
> Funny it seems, but by keeping its dreams,
> it learned to breathe fresh air.
> Long live the rose that grew from concrete
> when no one else ever cared. ~Tupac Shakur

On January 23, 2000, I was baptized in the Portland Church of Christ. That moment was nothing short of humbling. For so long, I had been running from the truth, burying my pain, and suppressing the weight of my sin. But my sins had carried me further than I ever thought possible – farther than I could have imagined.

As I stood there, on that stage, about to be baptized, flashes of my past came rushing back. I could still see myself searching for another grimy, soul-draining adult bookstore – each one a drug of its own. The memory of sitting in those disgusting, claustrophobic cubicles, filled with the stench of despair and sweaty disgust, haunted me. Those TVs, flickering with graphic images, were my escape, my temporary anaesthetic for a life lived without God.

I could still hear the roar of the engines, feel the rush of adrenaline from the late-night, high-speed drunken car races tearing through the city streets of Portland. All of it – my sins, my darkness – flashed before me as I stood there, waiting to be baptized.

In that moment, while most people were celebrating their new identity in Christ, I felt like the lowest form of a human. The cross wasn't just an abstract study for me – it wasn't merely a lesson learned. No, the cross was my only hope, my only salvation. Approaching that microphone to publicly proclaim Jesus as Lord, knowing how the feeling of abandonment made the moment more than a declaration. It was the most liberating moment of my life, a raw and soul-crushing release. All my shame, my past, my brokenness – all of it was washed away in that simple act. The weight of it all lifted, and I was a new person. Now my life mattered. The cross didn't erase my tears, but it gave them context, clarity, and a calling.

My tearful confession – *"Jesus is Lord"* – came out in a shaky voice, but it remains one of the most surreal moments of my life. The joy, the laughter, the sheer celebration over one sinner's repentance was overwhelming. To this day, when I replay that moment in my mind, it still feels like I was baptized yesterday.

> Who will cry for the little boy?
> Lost and all alone.
> Who will cry for the little boy?
> Abandoned without his own?
> Who will cry for the little boy?
> He cried himself to sleep.
> Who will cry for the little boy?
> He never had for keeps.
>
> Who will cry for the little boy?
> He walked the burning sand.
> Who will cry for the little boy?
> The boy inside the man.
> Who will cry for the little boy?
> Who knows well hurt and pain.
> Who will cry for the little boy?
> He died again and again.
>
> Who will cry for the little boy?
> A good boy he tried to be.
> Who will cry for the little boy?
> Who cries inside of me.

I stepped into leadership just three months after my baptism, super grateful and inspired to quickly emerge as an evangelistic force. I was placed in charge of directing the singles ministry – a group whose impact would extend beyond any other in the church. Clearly, this was God's grace, mercy, and humor all mixed together, utilizing the church's least faithful man to bring glory to Himself.

He didn't pick me because I was worthy – He picked me to show that grace still calls the unqualified, strengthens the broken, and rewrites the story for His glory. Yet, against this rising tide of ministry, two incidents would profoundly heal my heart and forever alter my understanding of grace.

The first of these life-changing moments came on my birthday when a particular song was sung – a version of Jim Gilbert's 1977 hymn that had been part of our worship many times before, but on that day, its message cut directly to the core of my wounded soul:

> *We love you with the love of the Lord,*
> *We love you with the love of the Lord,*
> *We see in you the glory of our King,*
> *And we love you with the love of the Lord.*

In that sacred moment, I was overwhelmed by a painful paradox. I had never believed I was worthy of God's love. How could they see in me the glory of our King? I had crucified Him with all my bitterness and anger, our King who was Jesus Christ, who had saved my soul. Did the disciples not know that I was, in my own eyes, the worst member of the church? The song shattered the dam I had built around my heart, and I broke down, crying uncontrollably for several minutes. Science might label this as a manifestation of pseudobulbar affect (a neurological condition that causes outbursts of uncontrolled or inappropriate crying), but to me, it was the unfiltered outpouring of a lifetime of hidden agony.

I wept for my mother's relentless struggle with drug addiction and her spiritual disconnection from God. I wept for the sexual abuse she endured by my grandfather. I wept for my brothers – scarred by abandonment, marred by gun violence, and consumed by drugs and alcohol. I wept for my younger brother, whose sexual confusion and painful journey into homosexuality after having been used as sexual collateral for my mother's drug use left him adrift in a storm of identity. I wept for the mystery of my unknown birth father, for my own inability to shield my mother from abuse from my stepdad, and for the sins that haunted me – my deviant use of pornography, my questionable choices, and the nine women I had persuaded to end their pregnancies. I questioned in despair, "Were those women female versions of me? Did I abuse them?" I wept for how I failed as a big brother and engaged in horrific sin with the second oldest. I wept for my worldly friends to scarred to admit they needed God, I wept for the nights spent in a dark, suffocating crack house at the tender age of 14, terrified beyond measure, and for the lonely, bitter streets of Portland, Oregon, and Vancouver, Washington where I wandered as a homeless teenager.

During my anguish, that familiar song became a conduit for truth. While many in attendance saw my tears as a simple expression of gratitude, a few discerning souls understood that my prolonged, soul-wrenching weeping was far deeper – a desperate cry for healing. There was a little boy hurting inside of the man. As **Psalm 34:18** assures us, *"The LORD is close to the brokenhearted and saves those who are crushed in spirit."*

After a few months, I found myself continually approached by a group of loving, older women in the church. Their gentle invitations – "Hey bro, let's talk" – resounded with sincere concern. Despite their warmth, I recoiled; the thought of unburdening my soul was terrifying. Their reassurances – "We know you're a leader in the church; you're doing awesome. Let us know when we can talk" – only intensified my inner turmoil. I was petrified to talk to those sisters. Deep down, a small, persistent voice whispered, "You're afraid to talk."

Eventually, I found the courage to share my painful past. As I told my story, their eyes filled with tears. Until then, I had convinced myself that my troubled upbringing was ordinary and not worth examining. But one sister, holding my hand, said, "Michael, you were abandoned and emotionally abused. Your brothers were sexually abused. You are a survivor of abuse and carry deep-seated anger. Your acting brilliance has roots in your past."

She spoke to me with compassion and conviction, breaking through my hardened heart. Living in self-deception, I realized my pain was proof of survival and needed healing through traditional discipling. Grace and truth provided healing without therapy, medication, or labels. That said, I hold deep respect for licensed counselling and professional therapy, especially when grounded in godly compassion, wisdom, and healing. Counselling can be a great tool to help with trauma healing and how to change one's thinking to refocus on God. Praise God, my counsellors were Christians!

Tears flowed as the sisters read these scriptures together:

> *The Lord is close to the brokenhearted and saves those who are crushed in spirit.* **(Psalm 34:18)**

> *God sets the lonely in families.* **(Psalm 68:6)**

> *The Spirit of the Sovereign LORD is on me, because the LORD has anointed me to proclaim good news to the poor. He has sent me to bind up the brokenhearted...* **(Isaiah 61:1)**

I displayed all four of the five stages of grief: Anger, Denial, Bargaining, and Depression. These signs can be found in *On Grief and Grieving,* written by Elisabeth Kubler-Ross & David Kessler. I left the meeting embracing the last stage: Acceptance. Each tear, each confession, was a step toward self-discovery – a powerful testimony that even in our darkest moments, God's love shines through, inviting us to embrace our brokenness and be made whole. In sharing my story, I started on the difficult yet liberating journey toward healing.

I walked away from that life-altering meeting telling myself the truth about my life. For the longest time, I had boasted about my ability not to cry. However, this clearly showed a deficit in the ability to love. Although I was baptized, I recounted the cost with myself. I saw how much pain I caused other people by not dealing with my heart. There was a renewed, strange confidence in accepting how lonely I was without God. I realized my mother's abuse toward me came from the abuse she suffered in her own life. There was a clarity and tingling sensation that is hard to put into words. I believe that tingling sensation was "truth" taking root in my heart. The tears I shed as I walked back home were the healing tears of truth.

John 20:25-27 states:

> *So the other disciples told him [Thomas], "We have seen the Lord!"*

> *But he said to them, "Unless I see the nail marks in His hands and put my finger where the nails were, and put my hand into His side, I will not believe."*

> *A week later His disciples were in the house again, and Thomas was with them. Though the doors were locked, Jesus came and stood among them and said, "Peace be with you!"*

> *Then He said to Thomas, "Put your finger here; see my hands. Reach out your hand and put it into my side. Stop doubting and believe."*

Thomas hadn't been there during Jesus's previous appearance to His disciples. In his absence, he likely wrestled with grief, doubt, and disillusionment, trying to make sense of the cross. Jesus, gentle, deliberate, and full of mercy, didn't shame him. He invited him to *"Put your finger here…"* In other words, He invited Thomas to touch the place where the pain was and look at the scars.

Jesus could have returned without scars, but He chose to keep them. He could have returned with glowing radiance, brilliance, untouched and flawless. This was not how He returned, however. Jesus decided to keep His scars.

Why? Because He was proud of them. Jesus knew His scars didn't scream defeat; they whispered victory. Scars say, "I have taken Satan's best punch and I'm still standing." When many would hide and cover over their scars, Jesus kept His uncovered and laid bare to show He was not ashamed of what He overcame.

When Jesus Christ shows us His wounds, this should dramatically change how we see ours. When Jesus shows us His truth, this is not just to inspire us but to dramatically change us. His truth should always transform our truth. His love wasn't theoretical. It bled, it broke, it scarred.

Life trains the teachable spirit to accept a profound truth: Pain is unavoidable. The only option we are given is what kind of pain we decide to endure. We may think it is selectable, but no matter the pain you choose, it is unavoidable in this life.

There is the pain that comes from suppressing our injuries or there is the pain of honesty and truth. One buries us slowly beneath silence, sadness, and undisclosed internal tears. The other burns in the beginning but sets us free. One pain torments us while the other transforms us.

There is the pain that comes from discipline and the pain that comes from regret. It is painful to say no to temptation, to be a man or woman of self-discipline. It is painful to uphold conviction, courage, and principle when it will cost you applause. It is painful to walk with integrity of heart when shortcuts are everywhere. Instant gratification is one of the modern drugs of choice. But the cancer of regret is more painful, the pain of knowing too late what could have been if you had said no, the torment of missed purpose, and the ache of wasted potential. The slow rot of a life built on compromise instead of character is always more painful.[4]

While the world taps into the vein of grievance and victimhood, true disciples learn to grieve with God, to name the wound and still stand proud with their scars. Satan's fist can become God's hand of freedom if we let the light in and let the tears out.

Tears are the path from wound to scar. They soften what bitterness tried to harden, the human heart. They break down walls and build up new beginnings. They speak when words cannot.

---

[4] **Hebrews 12:11; Proverbs 13:15; 25:28; Phil. 3:14.**

The truth is, we are not unemotional, passive observers of the pain in our lives. Life will not always be easy, but it will be meaningful. To walk in freedom, we must confront the shameful, painful, and buried truths that hold us hostage in the dark. When we finally stop running and begin releasing, something powerful happens. The tears that inevitably come during those moments do not weaken us, they awaken in us a well of inner strength, hidden behind years of silence, secrecy, or performance, dormant behind walls of self-protection. The tears we allow to flow become the ink that rewrites our narrative and signal to heaven that we are finally ready to heal.

God is not some distant, cold-hearted deity demanding that you, "just suck it up and get over it." He is not a cosmic killjoy trying to make you pretend your suffering never happened.

Psalm 56:8 (NLT) states,

> *You keep track of all my sorrows.*
> *You have collected all my tears in your bottle.*
> *You have recorded each one in your book.*

It is time to let go of the lie that tears make us weak. We need to soften that stiff upper lip and let go of the fear that crying makes us lose control. **Matthew 5:4** says, *"Blessed are those who mourn, for they will be comforted."*

We need to resist the temptation to be defined by our suffering and instead, be refined through it, shedding our tears of truth, not in defeat, but on the path to victory. We need to cry like Hannah, whose prayers were soaked in pain before her miracle was born, **(1 Samuel 1:10)** and weep like David, whose tears ran down his face as he cried out in the wilderness, but whose legacy God sealed as a man after His own heart. **(Psalm 6:6-7)**

Tears of truth are not just for sadness. They are the signposts of change. Our tears of truth can become prayers of passion. **Psalm 126:5** tells the Israelites, *"Those who sow in tears will reap with songs of joy."*

To the Abused, Abandoned, Ashamed, and Unaware:

You may carry deep and overwhelming scars: emotional, mental, spiritual, or even physical. There are scars that do not just mark your body but brand your heart.

Let me be crystal clear: you did not ask for what happened to you. You did not deserve the suffering. It was not your fault.

But God does not waste a hurt. He calls us to do what Jesus did after He died and was resurrected, His wounds closed but His scars remained as a testimony of love, survival, and glory: Square your shoulders, step out of your tomb, and walk with your head held high. You may be marked with scars, but you are still strong, perfected, and resurrected.

Your scars aren't signs of shame but of survival. They prove that abuse didn't destroy you. They declare, "I've been through hell – and I came out alive." They developed you. They testify that your tears didn't drown you.

I dare you: stop hiding your scars. Hold them up like Jesus did. Let the world see what God has brought you through. Because you never know … your scars might just become someone else's sermon. You are not alone, and you are not too broken to be used. You are beautiful amid the pain.

> Life's a book full of pain, But I turned the page.
> Scars on my soul, heart full of rage.
> Tears in my eyes, Cried through the night.
> Fire in my chest turned darkness to light.
> Tell every dream that I'm chasing, I'm on my way.
> Tell every lie I was told, not today.
> Tears of truth, yeah, the wounds still sore.
> But this wound has a name – It's called, "something more."
> Not there yet, but I'm built to rise,
> Hope in my heart, Truth in my eyes.
> Ignore the small limp, don't count me out
> Tears of truth, I'm on route.
>
> ~ Michael Williamson

In the end, it is not our strength that tells our story, it is our scars.

Chapter 3: Tears of Darkness

When the righteous cry for help, the Lord hears and delivers them out of all their troubles. The Lord is near to the brokenhearted and saves the crushed in spirit. **(Psalm 34:17-18 ESV)**

"The real man smiles in trouble, gathers strength from distress, and grows brave by reflection." ~Thomas Paine

In photography, a dark room is where negatives are developed into photographs. Old-school photography required film development, manual printing, and time. Photographers knew that light-sensitive materials must be placed in a dark room for them to be processed properly. Traditional film processing depends on the controlled chemical reduction of silver halide crystals, a reaction optimized in the carefully managed darkness of a darkroom.[5] In that space, the full character, the complete picture, and the true purpose of the image emerge. Before a photograph is delivered, it must be developed.

---

[5] "Film processing," Iowa State University, Center for Nondestructive Evaluation, accessed August 7, 2025, https://www.nde-ed.org/NDETechniques/Radiography/TechCalibrations/filmprocessing.xhtml.

In the same way, God typically develops our purpose in dark, painful, even miserable places – long before we ever see the light of healing and victory. This can involve significant trauma. The word "trauma" comes from the Greek word for *trauma, (τραύμα)*, meaning wound. The Greeks originally used the word trauma to describe physical injuries, yet now it encompasses emotional wounds resulting from abuse and neglect or tragic occurrences.

Before David was delivered and became king, he was developed in a dark room of spiritual abuse, death threats, and prolonged emotional and psychological torture at the hands of Saul. **(1 Samuel 19:1-3; 24:3-7)** David's dark room included the cave of Adullam, where he first fled. **(1 Samuel 22:1)** His psalms reveal his inner turmoil, confusion, anger, and anxiety. For example, in **Psalm 55:4-5 (ESV)** he writes, *"My heart is in anguish within me; the terrors of death have fallen upon me. Fear and trembling have come upon me, and horror has overwhelmed me."*

Other Biblical figures experienced trauma throughout their lives. Isaac was nearly sacrificed by his father on an altar to God, a memory that surely stayed with him all his life.

> *When they reached the place God had told him about, Abraham built an altar there and arranged the wood on it. He bound his son Isaac and laid him on the altar, on top of the wood. Then he reached out his hand and took the knife to slay his son.*
> **(Genesis 22:9-10)**

Facing death at the hands of a beloved and trusted family member can create deep psychological trauma.

Joseph endured betrayal from his brothers and suffered through false accusations, resulting in his imprisonment. *"So when the Midianite merchants came by, his brothers pulled Joseph up out of the cistern and sold him for twenty shekels of silver to the Ishmaelites, who took him to Egypt."* **(Genesis 37:28)** This unjust betrayal brought to Joseph was essentially emotional abuse from his family.

Job faced the loss of his children and wealth while his health deteriorated. **Job 1:20-21** states, *"At this, Job got up and tore his robe and shaved his head. Then he fell to the ground in worship and said: 'Naked I came from my mother's womb, and naked I will depart. The Lord gave and the Lord has taken away; may the name of the Lord be praised.'"* During his experience of extreme loss and physical agony, Job faced deep sorrow while also battling anger, depression, and trauma.

Naomi lost her husband and two sons, coming home to Israel a bitter woman, feeling abandoned and discouraged and doing everything she could to push other people away. She said to her daughters-in-law in **Ruth 1:20-21**, *"'Don't call me Naomi,' she told them. 'Call me Mara, because the Almighty has made my life very bitter. I went away full, but the Lord has brought me back empty. Why call me Naomi? The Lord has afflicted me; the Almighty has brought misfortune upon me.'"*

Even God's prophets faced moments of deep despair and hopelessness. Elijah, learning his life was in danger despite the huge victory he had just experienced for God, was overcome with exhaustion, discouragement, and suicidal thoughts. The Bible states, *"He travelled a day's journey into the wilderness, sat under a broom tree, and prayed that he might die, saying, 'It is enough! Now, Lord, take my life, for I am no better than my ancestors!'"* **(1 Kings 19:4)** Daniel was thrown in the darkness of the lion's den by the king he served faithfully. **(Daniel 6:16, 22)**

Finally, who can forget Jesus's moment at the Garden of Gethsemane as well as the trauma of the cross. He faced extreme physical, emotional, and spiritual suffering, being hated, rejected, betrayed, beaten, and finally executed. **Isaiah 53:3-5** states, *"He is despised and rejected by men, a man of sorrows and familiar with grief... He was wounded for our transgressions, bruised for our iniquities; the punishment for our peace was upon Him, and by His stripes, we are healed."*

Jesus carried the weight of human sin and suffered deeply. The tremendous suffering Jesus experienced caused His body to break down due to the stress. The pressure He faced in Gethsemane as He anticipated His betrayal and subsequent torture and crucifixion was so intense that He experienced hematidrosis and began sweating blood. **Luke 22:44** records this as *"And being in anguish, He prayed more earnestly, and His sweat was like drops of blood falling to the ground."* This is when stress triggers a rupture in blood vessels near sweat glands, resulting in blood mixing with sweat. The body's final reaction emerges when it undergoes intolerable suffering. Both military personnel experiencing extreme fear and death row inmates who face execution have displayed this same effect.

Many people think of Jesus's suffering in terms of the whip or the nails, but His ordeal began much earlier. The emotional torment of abandonment, betrayal, and the burden of sin overwhelmed Him before any physical harm was done. Scientific research indicates that emotional trauma can be more damaging and last longer than physical trauma. While both can have severe effects, psychological wounds often take longer to heal and can have a deeper impact on a person's overall mindset. Studies using MRI scans show that emotional pain (such as rejection, grief, or humiliation) activates the same brain regions as physical pain, particularly the anterior cingulate cortex and insula.[6]

This means that the brain processes heartbreak, betrayal, and loss in the same way as a physical injury, but without a straightforward healing process like a broken bone. We know Jesus had many of His bones broken. While physical wounds heal over time, emotional trauma can rewire the brain, leading to long-term issues described in psychological terms as PTSD, anxiety, and depression.[7] While it is hard to

[6] Naomi I. Eisenberger, Matthew D. Lieberman, Kipling D. Williams, "Does rejection hurt? An FMRI study of social exclusion," *Science* 302, no. 5653 (2003): 290-2, https://doi: 10.1126/science.1089134.

[7] Yehuda R, Hoge CW, McFarlane AC, Vermetten E, Lanius RA, Nievergelt CM, Hobfoll SE, Koenen KC, Neylan TC, Hyman SE., "Post-traumatic stress disorder." *Nature Review Disease Primers*, 1 (2015), https://doi: 10.1038/nrdp.2015.57.

imagine Jesus having PTSD, the point remains that His trauma was devastating.

His closest friends would abandon Him. His people would reject Him. He would bear the sins of the world – alone. This was not just physical pain. Human history has never seen a trauma more devastating and soul-crushing than this event.

Each of these men and women was marked by suffering before being place in a seat of authority or blessed with an incredible end to their story. God was shaping their fate long before they stepped into the light of deliverance – and He is doing the same in our lives today. Sometimes our current pain has a future purpose.

However, too many people remain in darkness – stuck in the process and refusing to let God shape them with suffering. It is good to be in God's dark room because what is fully developed in the dark will shine in the bright. However, if you never leave the dark room, you will never see the full picture of who you were meant to be because you will stay in a place designed for transformation rather than to be your destination. The trauma of the dark room can linger, far longer than any of us care to admit.

Unreleased trauma creates enduring internal burdens that persist within the body well beyond the end of the traumatic event. The trauma resembles an invisible scar left inside the body that never fully healed. It settles into muscles, breath, and bones, waiting for a chance to be released. You hear it in the bitter conversations here in London. You can feel it when it stops you from trusting anyone but your own opinions.

Unreleased pain does not simply fade away. Trauma does not disappear overnight. It digs in, it remains. Suppression can feel like survival because the body has memory. Peter Wentz says, "The hardest thing about depression is that it is addictive. It begins to feel uncomfortable not to be depressed. You feel guilty for feeling happy." Dr. Bessel van der Kolk in *The Body Keeps Score*, states that "Trauma is not just an event that took place sometime in the past. It is also the imprint left by that experience on mind, brain, and body." Trauma can be stored in the body, hidden in clenched fists, shallow breaths, and sleepless nights. It gets trapped in the nervous system, muscle memory, and even cellular expression. If it is not dealt with and released, it might become chronic stress, disease, anxiety, or depression – occasionally without you even remembering. In other words, trauma is like a bad experience that your body remembers, even if your mind doesn't.

It can be triggered when an authoritative voice conjures up old wounds buried in your heart. It can be triggered when pain feels normal and love feels uncomfortable. Moreover, it can influence future generations.

As disciples, it is essential to comprehend how these experiences shape us and how we, in turn, influence those around us. The saying "hurting people hurt people," highlights the cycle of pain and hurt that can perpetuate if left unaddressed. Modern science has now confirmed what many of us have known in our hearts: trauma is not just lived – it's also inherited from family to family through epigenetics, the biological changes in gene expression – whether genes are switched on or off – without altering the DNA sequence itself.

When there is trauma (abuse, war, famine, or chronic stress), it can cause chemical markers or tags to attach to DNA. These epigenetic markers can change gene function and can be passed down through generations. So, in essence you can be "tagged" by your grandmother's trauma, and it could be affecting your nervous system today. Likewise, our unhealed trauma can affect our children and generations after us.

A biological psychiatry study showed that children of Holocaust survivors had altered stress hormone profiles and heightened sensitivity to trauma.[8] Research by the National Institutes of Health (NIH) found that children of 9/11 survivors and combat veterans also have altered cortisol levels, suggesting inherited stress responses.[9] Studies on African American populations have discovered epigenetic markers resulting from ancestral trauma caused by slavery,

---

[8] Yehuda, R. et al, "Holocaust Exposure Induced Intergenerational Effects on FKBP5 Methylation," *Biological psychiatry*, vol 80, issue 5 (2016): 372-80.

[9] Yehuda, R. et al, "Transgenerational Effects of Posttraumatic Stress Disorder in Babies of Mothers Exposed to the World Trade Center Attacks during Pregnancy," *Journal of Clinical Endocrinology & Metabolism*, vol. 90, Issue 7 (2005), https://doi.org/10.1210/jc.2005-0550

racism, and segregation.[10] Finally, children born during the Dutch famine of 1944-5 had changed methylation patterns (epigenetic markers) affecting metabolism and stress resistance.[11]

Generations before epigenetics made the news, Scripture taught us about generational sin, iniquity, and consequences. In **Exodus 20:5**, it says, *"I, the Lord your God, am a jealous God, punishing the children for the sins of the fathers to the third and fourth generation."* However, the Bible also teaches us the way to escape. **Galatians 3:13** states, *"Christ redeemed us from the curse of the law by becoming a curse for us."* We may inherit pain, trauma, and spiritual patterns, but we do not need to hand them on. As a disciple, the curse can be cut, and a new family line of blessing and healing can begin.

The problem is our own impatience. We want digital discipleship, in which there is no patience, process, depth, or real connection. Another problem is overemphasizing the barriers to growth. God is in control, but on some levels, so are we. If we dwell too much on the barriers to growth, we begin to see life through a lens of media and social limitations, not Godly merit or transformation. We also lose

---

[10] Kaufman J, et al, "Transgenerational Inheritance and Systemic Racism in America." *Psychiatric Research and Clinical Practice*, vol 5, no. 2 (2023):60-73. https://doi.org/10.1176/appi.prcp.20220043.

[11] Heijmans BT, et al, "Persistent epigenetic differences associated with prenatal exposure to famine in humans," *Proceedings of the National Academy of Sciences of the United States of America*, Vol 105, no 44 (Nov. 4, 2008): 17046-17049, https://doi.org/10.1073/pnas.0806560105.

personal agency. When pain is crowned as our identity and hardship is enshrined as a heritage, we quietly abdicate responsibility for our future. Society has done a marvelous job over the last decade of training those living in the western world to idolize injuries. We start waiting for healing to show up by proxy, waiting for society to fix us, or for others to notice our misfortune. Soon afterwards, we expect others to rescue us. Before long, we become society's new little darling: the Victim.

I've seen this narrative play out powerfully in my own community: the African American community. Much of the dialogue around slavery in America, while necessary, has morphed into a political doctrine, one that excuses the present by eternalizing the past.

We force-feed the public broken men like George Floyd as moral icons for young black boys to look up to. We unconsciously condition young white boys to think they have a "white privilege," when the truth is that no one has "privilege" other than Jesus. While George Floyd's death was tragic, sainthood should not be based on instability, godless character, and delinquency.

Meanwhile, history itself is revised through the lenses of American chattel slavery, ignoring the broader and older, global context. Slavery has existed in every corner of the world since Pharaoh enslaved Israel. It is a sin issue not a skin issue.

What is more rarely discussed is this: North African Barbary pirates enslaved over one million white Europeans between the 16th and 18th centuries. These included Englishmen, French, Italians, and even Americans. According to historian Robert Davis in *Christian Slaves, Muslim Masters*, the number of white Europeans enslaved by Barbary raiders between 1500 and 1800 potentially rivals or exceeds the number of Africans enslaved in North America during the same time period. Without a doubt, however, chattel slavery in America was more sinister, as the word "chattel" comes from the French word "chatel," which means "cattle," highlighting the degradation brought upon African Americans caught in this type of slavery.

However, the question is why the slavery by Barbary pirates is missing from most school textbooks? The answer is simple: dependency is profitable when government replaces the God of the Bible as the god of our hearts. If you can convince a people that they are permanently oppressed, you can control their vote, their hope, and their agency. Victimhood has become the most valuable currency in the world. However, it's a counterfeit currency that will cost you your character if you buy into the narrative.

Many of the barriers we obsess over are abstract idols – crafted not by God but by a world addicted to the glorification of pain and the worship of wounds. Satan loves this. He cannot change your past, so he tries to chain your future – to a narrative-driven wound badge. When you define yourself as a victim, even opportunities begin to feel like entitlement tickets instead of stepping-stones from God to make you a better person.

God allowed me to be developed in the darkness to shine in the light. The darkness of abandonment, being left in a house unfit for human life, became God's developing room. Looking at the darkness in my mother and witnessing the generational cycles of hurt in my family, I knew I had to get out. But before I could get out, I needed to go through the trauma of God's dark room.

One of the deepest darkrooms in my development was 13th Street, a place where shadows loomed heavy, where difficulty always seemed to call my name, and where every step down the block felt like a slow walk through a thornbush. This was the street on which I grew up in Vancouver. Yet, even growing up on a street full of evil and darkness, God was at work. He was moulding me, pressing me, chiselling away at the very core of my sinful nature.

It was during a turbulent time when my mother was abruptly arrested – a moment that marked the birth pains of her completely abandoning us about a year later. With our world turned upside down, we were forced to live with my uncle's girlfriend, who stepped in to play the role of "mom" for a few, long, agonizing months. She tried to act like a mother, but it was survival at best.

We were still on 13th street, and if you know anything about 13th street, it was more than an address. Survivors of this street earned a kind of badge of honor that represented fierce loyalty like gang members defending their territory and hooligans standing by their postal code. Years later, even as adults, we'd end a hard truth with "… Like when we were on 13th street." It wasn't nostalgia – it was code for grit and determination. It was a verbal scar that needed no explanation.

My uncle's girlfriend was far from comforting. She carried an air of cruelty and disdain, speaking down to us in hushed, venomous tones when she thought no one was watching. Every gesture and word dripped with spite, and she made it abundantly clear that defiance would not be tolerated in "her house." To me it wasn't "her house." I would think to myself, "This is our house, lady. I know things are a bit broken, but we are the pieces left behind. This is still our house!"

Her threats of physical harm were not empty promises – they loomed over us constantly, a grim reminder that in a fractured home, militant obedience was our only means of survival. My brothers took pride in how tough their older brother was, but this lady scared me. She was tall, imposing, and seemed to look through your soul with her eyes. I cried when no one was watching, especially my younger brothers.

The vast difference between our mother's nurturing meals and the bland food we endured when she wasn't there served as a painful reminder of our loss. My mother's extraordinary culinary skills produced dishes that matched the expertise of a Michelin-starred chef while spreading nourishment and soulful love throughout our home. Despite our financial struggles and reliance on food stamps, her meals were what made everything better. Every meal served more than mere sustenance; it delivered heartfelt messages of love and worth in every bite, which declared, "You matter." Many poor families communicate their love through food.

But the woman who temporarily took over our care served food that was not only unpalatable but also a constant, painful reminder that we were living in a world far removed from the love and warmth of my mother's home. Macaroni, green beans, corn, tuna and tomatoey pepper soup still sounds repugnant.

To make matters even worse, the air was often tainted with the disgusting stench of crackpipe smoke. At first, I thought it was just odd-smelling cigarettes – the smoke was thicker and more synthetic. But soon, I realized the truth: they were getting high while babysitting us. In the cramped, grimy bathroom, the mingled odor of crack cocaine – smoked by both her and my uncle – seeped into every corner of our temporary refuge. This is why we were always itching our skin. The combination of the bitter food and overwhelming smell of drugs transformed our days into an assault on every sense, etching memories of neglect and chaos that would linger long into my adulthood.

It felt like an eternity until my mother was released from jail, even though it was only a few months. We cried tears of joy when she returned home. Things went back to "normal" for a while until the next family grenade went off. By then, I had learned not to trust peace. It felt too painful to believe in peace when chaos and tears had always been the norm. Soon,

I would face the real darkness of abandonment – not for three months, but forever.

Before that, I was just one of the 13th street boys. So many dark stories happened on that street. A close friend once confided in me, "I can still smell her disgusting cigarette breath. I was only twelve, and my mother used to pimp me out to her female friends." He told this story as if it were nothing – as if he were not confessing horrific sexual abuse. But I knew better, and this was just one of the many stories of his life.

Another friend told me about the secret life of his uncle. The same uncle that the neighborhood knew as "the man" who was secretly having sex with other men, and worse, had touched my friend as well. His uncle was very friendly with all of us. I liked him because he was muscular, fit, and stylish. However, this story made me realize why my friend hated him – because how could you hate your uncle?

A full-body naked male family member would stroll through the living room of the crack house I called home. His own cousin was waiting for him in the bedroom when he returned. They carried on having the relationship for weeks. Even as a child this felt weird. My mother, his older sister, approved of these actions because they took place in our home's spare room. As time passed, I observed my mother fall deeper into her addiction, which buried her love for anything other than herself. Each time she got high, the nurturing side of her as a mother was destroyed. The drugs stole the identity of my mother, and I longed for her to return.

Darkness lived all over 13th street, but we did not know it as kids. Even just recently I found out that another 13th street boy (now man) has died, a good friend. As I write this book I want to show respect to Andre Perry, Trevor Burnell, Steve Peirce, Kevin Madden, Kenneth Atkins (Snapper), Jason, Jerald, Tasha, and Mikey McClinton, Michele, Monica, Deangelo, Stevie Borowick, Saul Tamu, Tod McClaskey, Dong (who visited the block), and many others.

Tears often flow for several reasons, and on 13th street those reasons were far darker than anyone could have imagined. This ordinary neighborhood harbored secrets that would make even the strongest souls weep.

There was a facade of normalcy. To the casual observer, we all played basketball at King's elementary school during the daytime, and we played moon tag at night. Most neighbors exchanged pleasantries, and families attended church on Sundays. However, behind closed doors and in the darkness, a sinister reality affected many of the kids.

Despite her reputation for toughness, a young girl endured unimaginable horrors without making a sound. The community revered her stepfather as "Big T" because he played the role of helpful handy man and devoted father while also being well-known for his humor. But his weird smile, perfect for a Tarantino film, hid a monstrous secret, years of sexual abuse against the girl he was meant to protect. The tears this young girl shed were born of fear, pain, and betrayal.

A boy known for his fighting prowess succumbed to the weight of his abuse, his tears of despair leading to a tragic end. He developed a drug addiction to cocaine and other hard narcotics. He also committed suicide after it was exposed that he was abused by his father. Another child, abused by his stepfather, channelled his pain into combat sports, his tears of anger fuelling his training. One boy's curiosity led him to discover his mother's hidden stash of graphic material, setting him on a path of sexual depravity and emotional turmoil as an adult. This boy learned as a child to seek connection and affection through shame. I can relate to this boy, because this boy is me.

I can say I survived what made most people snap. However, sometimes, someone would speak too casually about going through something challenging, and a deeper voice – the voice of someone who really lived it – would cut in and say, "Yeah, but that wasn't like 13th Street." And the room would fall quiet because we knew. Thirteenth Street made us who we are. It scarred us. It shaped a collective identity inside of us all forged in fire. On some days when I get discouraged, because of persecution or difficulty, I preach to myself. I stand tall despite the weight I carry, and I whisper to myself: "Just like when we were on 13th Street."

The narrative of Thirteenth Street exposes the hidden agony that numerous individuals experience. Every 68 seconds, another American falls victim to sexual assault. Approximately one out of every six American women has endured the trauma of an attempted or completed rape during her lifetime, with 14.8% experiencing completed assaults and 2.8% facing attempted ones. Similarly, about 3% of American men – equivalent to 1 in 33 – have encountered attempted or completed rape in their lifetimes. Disturbingly, from 2009 to 2013, Child Protective Services agencies substantiated or found compelling evidence indicating that 63,000 children annually were victims of sexual abuse. Among victims under the age of 18, 34% of those subjected to sexual assault and rape are under the age of 12, while a staggering 66% are between the ages of 12 and 17. One in five children in Europe are victims of some form of sexual violence. Two out of ten women in Europe have experienced physical and/or sexual violence from a friend.[12]

Childhood experiences like these and the ones lived by those on Thirteenth Street can leave a mark that reaches much further than the experience itself. Many survivors continue to live with their trauma into their adult years. There can be an evolution of childhood tears to adult struggles for many. Drug use serves as a method of pain relief for many survivors, resulting in tears of addiction. Hurt transforms into aggression and violent behavior, bringing tears of rage. There are also tears of shame – a profound sense of guilt because of their experiences.

Thirteenth Street was engulfed in darkness, yet a ray of hope persisted in some. Survivors managed to escape their circumstance while carrying the emotional scars from the

---

[12] Rachel E. Morgan, and Jennifer L Truman, "Criminal Victimization, 2019," Department of Justice, Office of Justice Programs, Bureau of Justice Statistics, National Crime Victimization Survey, accessed August 7, 2025, https://bjs.ojp.gov/content/pub/pdf/cv19.pdf.

experience. They learned to cry tears of healing as they faced their past while searching for support. Others found liberation from harmful habits and shed tears of relief. Finally, survivors began to create better futures for themselves and shed tears of joy. Their story demonstrates how humans can remain resilient even under challenging circumstances. Tears may originate from suffering, yet they also can simultaneously mark the start of healing and transformation. We begin our path of empathy and change by recognizing why we cry.

The Bible also serves as a comforting refuge when we experience tears of pain. **Revelation 21:4** contains the promise that He will remove every tear from our eyes. Death will cease to exist, along with mourning and all crying and pain. Likewise, **Psalm 34:18** tells us that the Lord supports those who feel broken-hearted while saving people who suffer from crushed spirits. These words provide hope and healing during our darkest moments. **Psalm 23:4** states, *"I walk through the darkest valley but fear no evil because you accompany me, and your rod and staff comfort me."*

Greater challenges lead to more magnificent victories. Only when something is hard to obtain do we truly appreciate its worth. I admire those who can maintain their composure under pressure while extracting strength from adversity through thoughtful reflection. People with limited courage easily give up but those whose hearts remain steadfast while their conscience supports their actions will keep their principles to their dying day.

Trauma does not have to stay trapped inside or linger into future generations. It can be released, and I have found three ways of doing so. Exercise is the first. Moving my body helped me move my pain. This is not just a metaphor but neurology in motion. With every run, every push, every effort, I fought to free myself from the grip of my past. Scientifically, exercise gets rid of cortisol, a stress hormone, while increasing the body's natural happy hormones, called endorphins. Dr. Bessel van der Kolk emphasizes movement-based therapies like yoga, stating, "Physical movement allows people to regain a sense of safety, agency, and presence in their bodies." A study showed that exercise significantly reduced symptoms of anxiety, depression, and PTSD.[13]

The second way was through breathing. Deep, intentional breaths reminded me that I was alive, that I had control, and that I could breathe in peace and breathe out pain. Dr. Mike Dow, in his book, *The Brain Fog Fix*, and other works talks about vagus nerve stimulation through slow, deep breathing to shift from fear-based subconscious programming to calm, conscious awareness. Controlled breathing has also been shown to reduce PTSD symptoms and improve emotional regulation.[14]

---

[13] Hegberg NJ, Hayes JP, Hayes SM, "Exercise Intervention in PTSD: A Narrative Review and Rationale for Implementation," *Front Psychiatry*, vol 10, no 133 (2019), https://doi: 10.3389/fpsyt.2019.00133.

[14] Seppälä EM, et al, "Breathing-based meditation decreases posttraumatic stress disorder symptoms in U.S. military veterans: a randomized controlled longitudinal study." *Journal of Traumatic Stress*, vol 27, issue 4 (2014):397-405, https://doi: 10.1002/jts.21936.

Another way is through expression, or in other words, talking it out. Neuroscience shows that narrating your experience – in therapy, journaling, or by speaking to a trusted community of people like the church – restores logic to emotional chaos. The rational part of our brain, the prefrontal cortex, is thus engaged. When we develop the courage to put our pain into spoken words, this can happen.

The final but most powerful release was crying. For years I held them back, thinking tears were a sign of weakness. But I have learned that tears heal. Dr. Mike Dow also discusses how emotional release through tears can rewire emotional patterns by unlocking the limbic system where trauma is stored.

How Trauma Leaves the Body

Movement (Exercise)	Expression (Talking It Out)	Crying (Tears of Release)
• Discharges stored trauma • Resets stress response • Activates healing through motion	• Restores logic to emotion • Engages rational brain (prefrontal cortex) • Heals through verbal processing	• Releases cortisol & stress hormones • Triggers parasympathetic response • Emotional detoxification

Scientists have confirmed the idea that the way forward to healing is through allowing ourselves to cry. Dr. William H. Frey II, renowned as a neuroscientist and biochemist, exhaustively explored the composition of tears, cementing his status as a leading authority in the field. His groundbreaking investigations into emotional tears propose that crying acts as a physiological mechanism for the body to expel stress hormones.

Dr. Ad Vingerhoets, a prominent figure in emotional crying research, has meticulously examined tears intricate physiological and psychological underpinnings. With a plethora of scholarly contributions spanning numerous publications and books, Dr. Vingerhoets' work explains various facets of tears, from exploring gender disparities in crying to dissecting the evolutionary origins and social functions inherent in this universal human phenomenon.

What has been discovered is that the act of crying serves to process our emotions beyond mere expression. There are three types of tears: basal, reflex, and psychic. Basal tears are tears that moisturize our eyes and shield them from environmental irritants. Reflex tears are those that form as the body responds to stimuli such as onions and dust. Psychic tears are produced when people feel happiness, sadness, or overwhelming emotions.

Psychic tears enable us to navigate complicated emotions while helping us to accept challenging realities. Have you ever noticed how much better you feel after a good cry? That's not just your imagination. Crying triggers the release of oxytocin and endorphins, feel-good chemicals that help alleviate both physical and emotional pain. It's nature's own painkiller and are a natural conduit to recovery.

In addition, during emotional distress, human tears help remove dangerous stress hormones such as cortisol from the body, which otherwise can cause serious health problems not easily seen by the human eye. Elevated cortisol can cause brain damage, weaken the immune system, or increase blood pressure. Crying is not weakness but the body's literal detox system for emotional overload. Crying calms the nervous system, slows the heart rate, and activates the parasympathetic response (rest-and-digest). Tears are like God's built-in detox plan for the nervous system.

When people hold back their tears, pretending everything is well, they add unnecessary stress to their minds and hearts. Dr. Conti, a leading expert in trauma healing who has worked with celebrities like Lady Gaga and Kim Kardashian, explains the impact of suffering on human lives. He describes trauma and suffering as an unseen pandemic that touches almost fifty percent of the population. Research shows that unresolved bitterness and emotional trauma leads to multiple physical health problems like Parkinson's disease and heart conditions.

Crying decreases manganese levels in the body because this mood-affecting mineral exists at much higher levels in tears than in the blood serum. High amounts of manganese in the body may lead to anxiety as well as aggressive behavior and irritability. Manganese is like a special spice my mother used to season chicken – just a tiny bit made the chicken tase right. Adding a little to our brains helps us think right and feel right. Too much Manganese is like adding a jar of cayenne to your food. It ruins the meal and makes the brain super anxious and worried.

Tears also help the brain have a chemical reset. They activate the parasympathetic nervous system (rest and digest mode) to help you avoid numbing out or having a major outburst from built-up stress. Shedding a few tears from grief will lead to comfort before you collapse. If you have been crying lately, this is an excellent sign that your body is healing.

These scientific findings confirm what the Bible has stated for thousands of years about the value that pain and suffering can have in our lives. As disciples of Jesus, we are continually confronted with moments that call for healing. **Psalm 103:2-3** states, *"Praise the Lord my soul and forget not all His benefits – who forgives all your sins and heals all your diseases."* **Psalm 46:1** declares, *"God is our refuge and strength, an ever-present help in trouble."* **Psalm 18:11** adds *"He made darkness His covering, His canopy around Him – the dark rain clouds of the sky."* Meanwhile, **Psalm 73:26** expresses, *"My flesh and my heart may fail, but God is the strength of my heart and my portion forever."* God tells us more than once to give Him all our anxieties because of His love for us. **(Psalm 55:22; Phil. 4:6; 1 Peter 5:6-7)** The result of not avoiding our pain but bringing it to God is peace. **(Phil. 4:7; John 14:27; 2 Tim 1:7; 1 Peter 5:10)**

Therapists often promote crying during sessions because it serves as a healthy emotional release mechanism. For many, tears indicate progress because they show that the client is engaging with and working through suppressed emotions.

Dr. Orloff, a distinguished psychiatrist and prolific author, has delved extensively into the intricate interplay between emotions and physical well-being. Her seminal work, *Emotional Freedom*, profoundly explores tears' therapeutic ability. It advocates for embracing one's emotional spectrum, including the act of shedding tears, as a vital conduit for healing and personal growth. In addition, Dr. Alexa Miller, an accomplished psychologist, brings forth a nuanced understanding of the psychological dimensions inherent in crying and emotional expression. She illuminates tears' multifaceted social and cultural significance through her work, explaining how crying is a profound form of interpersonal communication and emotional release across diverse contexts. **Psalm 34:18** states, *"The Lord is close to the brokenhearted and saves those who are crushed in spirit."* Here, the Psalmist assures us that God draws near to those who are hurting, offering comfort and salvation to the brokenhearted. Tears are also a signal to others that we need help.

The Greek word that is most often used in the New Testament to express healing is *therapuo*, appearing 42 times. This word means healing, restoration, and service. Perhaps Jesus, in **Luke 9:1-2**, understood that the disciples were not merely given the power to "heal" but more profoundly they were being equipped to provide therapy to wounded souls as an act of service to God. *Therapuo* can also be rendered as "therapeutic." Preaching the gospel becomes an act of administering therapy to the sick and a means of personal restoration for the administrator. It is not the healthy that need a doctor but the sick. **(Matthew 9:12)** Dare we say that we find healing ourselves in healing others?

So let those tears flow, whether tears of joy or sadness. As disciples we must refuse to define ourselves by chains, scars, or systemic limitations. We must refuse to be defined by injuries in the kingdom or out of the kingdom. We are not merely survivors – we are sons and daughters of the Most High God. Jesus asked the paralyzed man in **John 5:6:** *"Do you want to get well."* In the same way, God asks us: "Do you want to stay stuck? Or do you want to stand up and walk?" Accept your tears as they cleanse your daily existence and show the brilliance of your inner self.

Also understand that our harrowing experiences in life can result in us developing greater strength and resilience. I know they did for me. Every hill I had to climb, every sudden turn of events in my life, and all the challenging terrain, trained me for the privilege of sharing the gospel. My trials trained me for the test as I became better equipped because I suffered and overcame. God allowed trials in my life not to expose my shame and weakness, but to expose strengths I did not know were there. I would never have thought a man raised around the horrific things that I was, would be a man God was preparing to stand in the gap for world evangelism.

It's about replacing victimhood with victory, not by minimizing the dark moments in life, in history, or in any other sphere, but by growing despite them.

"There is no distress so complete but that even in the most critical moments the inexplicable sunrise of hope is seen in its depths." ~Victor Hugo

Chapter 3: Tears of Darkness

Chapter 4: Changing Your Mind about Changing Your Mind

Living in Europe for the past 15 years, I've noticed a persistent cultural myth that people cannot change their thinking. "This is just how I've always thought," or "That's just me."

That's only true when people refuse to acknowledge their feelings. You cannot change your mind until you're willing to let your heart break open. And sometimes, the fastest way to the heart is through a tear.

The Greeks called it *metanoia* – a complete reversal of the direction and change of mind. *Metanoia* is not about feeling excessive regret, but repentance. The Greeks understood repentance turned you from one world of thinking to another, like a London train line reversing its course to the sounds of the conductor saying, "this train terminates here."

In today's circles modern-day scientists call it neuroplasticity – the ability of the human brain to rewire itself. The brain can rewire itself by forming new paths and connections, leading to new thoughts and new decision.

So, change is not only possible because God is in control, but change is also possible because you are in control of your mind. You're in control of a changing your mind. Tears offer you a mental baptism, which becomes a bridge to new thinking.

Here's a simple (slightly painful) example:

When we lived in Los Angeles, our staff meetings were in El Segundo. I always drove the same route from Hollywood – 101 to the 110. Everyone knows one thing for sure if you've ever driven 101. It's not a freeway; it's a parking lot with billboards and palm trees. I was in concrete-purgatory – miserable, stuck, because let's face it, this is always how we got there. This route was fixed in my brain.

But one day, I took Sunset Boulevard instead–no GPS, just a hunch and a prayer. To my surprise, not only did I avoid traffic, but I also arrived quicker. I had committed myself to a longer, stressful route because it was sadly "all I knew."

That's exactly how the brain works, my friend. Your mental 101 may be anger, apathy, panic, pride, shame, or bitterness, or good old-fashioned overthinking. Trust me, taking new paths can create a new peace of mind, and godly mental muscle memory.

Several years later, God blessed us with the planting of the London International Christian Church, and I developed a similar, hard-wired mental routine. I always took the Circle Line from Baker Street to King's Cross, made the transfer to the Northern Line, and presto, I was at home in Camden

Town! That was my default pathway every time: quick, predictable, familiar, encrypted into my neural GPS! Not bad for an American figuring out Europe.

Then, out of nowhere, it happened like a car crash! Bang! A wild snowstorm shut down the city and several train lines!

I got lucky because the Circle Line dropped me off at King's Cross as usual, but the Northern Line was suspended. So, I waited. And waited. And waited some more. Frustrated, I boarded the Circle Line again, convinced I'd find a way. Every time the train conductor told me we were headed north, I got hopeful. Two hours later I was still circling like the Israelites, **(Numbers 32:13)** learning that sometimes God lets us walk in circles until our old thinking dies off.

Comically, I finally understood why it was called the Circle Line.

Totally dejected, I got off the Circle Line at Baker Street – the mentally familiar spot at that time –and I start walking. In the freezing snow, feet numb, hands frozen, hungry as a hostage, I trudged another 45 minutes on foot to Camden Town. I later realized… my flat was a five-minute walk from King's Cross Station.

I wasn't trapped by trains that day. I was trapped by habit. I was stuck thinking that the route I always took was the only option.

And that's precisely how neuroplasticity works.

When you repeat specific thoughts, ideas, and behaviors, they form pathways in your brain. This is great if they are positive in nature, but sadly, we can stay stuck on the ineffective pathways, or stuck in these negative thoughts, so much so that we start believing there is no other way. These thoughts become our default, turning us into "default disciples." "This is just the way I am; I've always been an overthinker." The truth is that we do not have to believe everything we think.

Neuroplasticity suggests that there are alternative routes you can create in your mind, which are shorter, more practical, and have less congestion and traffic. If crowded London tube rides always put you on the road to "rage," neuroplasticity suggests there are alternative paths you can take.

Science once believed that the human brain was fixed as soon as it was born, that essentially, you're stuck with the brain God gave you; however, this is not true. This "fixed brain" thinking dominated scientific thought for years. But it has now been revealed that well into your old age, neuroplasticity can still occur. It's called "plastic brain" versus the "fixed brain" thinking.

There are two forms of neuroplasticity: "structural plasticity," which changes the brain's physical size, and "functional plasticity," the brain's ability to reassign functions from a damaged area to a new, undamaged area in the brain. So, neuroplasticity gives you the power to influence your brain's functionality and size! You can change your behavior, and you can change your mind.

Now I must be fair, neuroplasticity can work negatively as well, reinforcing specific negative pathways in the brain, but the good news is it can be reversed. When you start focusing on the positive pathways the brain is now taking, you can strengthen the mind's ability to be positive. What you think you start to believe, and what you believe you start to live.

Now, let's bring this full circle (pun intended), connecting the power of tears and changing your mind. We will discuss how tears don't just express what's broken; they also reveal a new layer of growth. They make space for what's about to be built. Dare we say, when weeping ends, mind change begins. So, tears are not only a liquid substance that falls from our eyes, but they are also the liquid drops that land at the crossroads of something brand new, a changed brain, and a changed mind.

As we step into this next chapter – "Changing Your Mind About Changing Your Mind" – we move forward not with dry eyes and clinical logic, but with a hopeful realization: "I'm not stuck." Old paths, old thoughts, may be easier and familiar, but God, through this book, is inviting me to take a new path and a new route. I can change my mind about changing my mind.

What if I told you that hitting the gym five days a week could increase the size of your biceps? What if I said that with a strict, concentrated regime of heavy lifting you could build bulging abs as a single man? What if I also told you that your dad bod was not a life sentence, that through faithfully hitting the gym you could tighten your core, build your chest, and convict your teenage son this summer at the beach?

Ladies, what if I told you that you could reshape your entire physical body, yes dramatically, through disciplined, consistent effort? That you would produce real results, not just changing your appearance with filters for Instagram, Tik Tok, or YouTube?

These statements sound like obvious truths to a generation that has turned gym mirrors and bathroom lighting into selfie studios.

What might shock you is that science has now revealed that you can change the size of your brain through focused, positive thinking. Getting a big head can become a compliment for the first time in history!

Disciples know that **Romans 12:2** states, *"Be transformed by the renewing of your mind."* What science is now uncovering is that this is a physical, not just spiritual, reality. Dr. Mike Dow, in *Healing the Broken Brain* and *The Brain Fog Fix* says: "The subconscious mind can change your brain." In other words, your mind is not stuck. Your brain is not fixed. You can reshape the way you think. By doing that, you reshape the structure of your brain.

Most of your decisions and thoughts – blinking, breathing, scratching an itch – happen subconsciously. That part of your brain works like a hard drive: it stores habits, patterns, and programmed responses, many of which are built through past trauma and repeated negativity.

Our negative thinking, thoughts like "I'll never get better," "I always mess up," "No one will ever love me," or "I'm broken," are not just passing thoughts. They may be neural pathways in your brain, carved by repetition and pain. So you can program yourself to be negative!

Twenty-five years in the ministry have shown me that thoughts are not facts. This truth might seem simple, but it's revolutionary when we are suffering. Pain whispers thoughts in our mind like "I always mess up," "No one will ever love me," and "I'll never change." Pain can also be a megaphone: "You'll never be good enough, you don't deserve peace, chaos is your home." However, these are not facts. They are thoughts, distorted, wounded thoughts shaped by fear, failure, injury, and fatigue. While they may feel real, they are not true. Consider the title of the book: *Don't Believe Everything You Think.*

Yet the Bible also states: *"As a man thinketh in his heart, so is he."* **(Proverbs 23:7)** What you believe can shape the man or woman you become. So what that tells us is that the battle truly is in our minds. Our thoughts are not facts, but God's thoughts are facts. That's why **Romans 12:2** says, *"Be transformed by the renewing of your mind,"* and **Proverbs 1:7** tells us, *"The fear of the Lord is the beginning of knowledge."* The foundation of true knowledge is knowing God. **Colossians 2:3** states, *"... in Christ are hidden all the treasures of wisdom and knowledge."*

You do not have to remain enslaved by what you have suffered. You are not defined by your darkest thoughts. If you are in Christ, you have the mind of Christ. **(1 Cor 2:16)** God has now given you a new perspective, a righteous reality, and a renewed, realistic, responsible identity. All healing begins when you decide to stop believing the "thoughts" in your head and start believing the truth in the Bible.

Those negative patterns of thinking can be rewired, and it starts with conscious choice.

Changing the subconscious mind requires conscious effort and input, which isn't easy initially. This is why we must read the Bible daily and listen to positive music daily. We need to feed our brain good things. Just as consistent lifting in the gym builds muscles, the more you lift those new thoughts, the stronger they become. Habits get stronger with age.

Every time you speak Scripture out loud, replace a lie with God's truth, choose forgiveness over offense, break a negative thinking cycle with positive affirmations, and praise instead of panic, you are changing your brain's structure. You're reducing fear, shrinking shame and strengthening peace, focus, and resilience.

The chart below shows how neuroplasticity allows the brain to change.

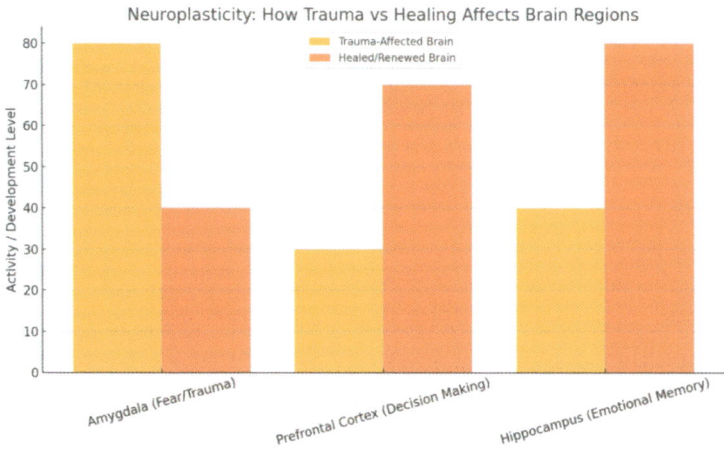

Neuroplasticity: How Trauma vs Healing Affects Brain Regions

The Trauma-Affected brain shows increased activity in the amygdala (seat of fear and anxiety) and reduced development in areas like the prefrontal cortex (rational thinking, impulse control) and hippocampus (emotional regulation, memory). On the other hand, the Healed/Renewed Brain, through prayer, breathwork, openness, forgiveness, reflection, and reading Scripture, shows shrinking fear centers and strengthening of peace and decision-making regions.

In the chart below, we can again see the difference between a Trauma-Affected Brain and a Healed/Renewed Brain, highlighting the changes in the amygdala, prefrontal cortex, and hippocampus.

Comparison of Trauma-Affected and Healed Brains

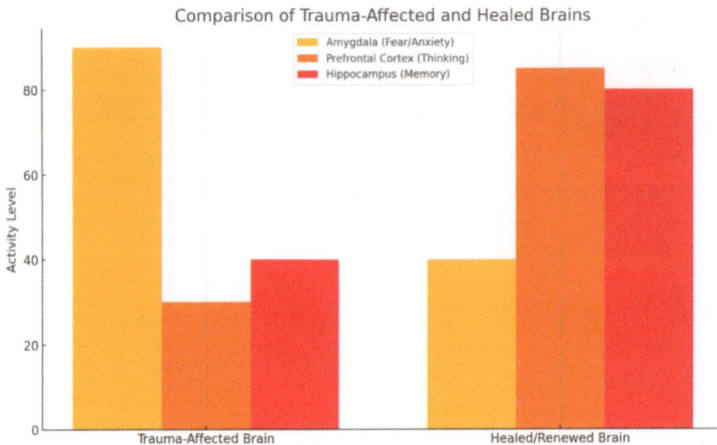

Dr. Timothy Jennings, a Christian psychiatrist, neurobiologist, and author states, "Every thought you have changes your brain's structure. Thinking God's thoughts actually calms the fear circuits and enhances love circuits."[15] Just as the diagram above shows, he teaches that believing in a loving, trustworthy God will strengthen the brain's prefrontal cortex (seat of self-control and peace) and decrease the amygdala (fear center). His study shows how unbiblical ideas about God (that He is legalistic and angry) can actually create anxiety and brain dysfunction, and how believing in the loving God of the Bible will transform the mind, heart, and brain.

Dr. Mike Dow states, "You can train your brain to heal itself. Your habits, your thoughts, your diet, your movement – they

---

[15] Timothy Jennings, *The God-Shaped Brain: How Changing Your View of God Transforms Your Life* (IVP, 2017).

can all rewire your brain for peace, purpose, and power."[16] Dr. Caroline Leaf puts it this way, "As your consciously direct your thinking, you can literally change the physical structure of your brain."[17] Her *21-Day Brain Detox* is rooted in both Scripture and neuroscience, showing that thoughts are real, physical things that take up mental space and can be rewired.

Another clinical neuroscientist, brain imaging expert, and practicing Christian, Dr. Daniel Amen states, "Your brain is the organ of loving, learning, and behaving. Change your brain, and you change your life."[18] Amen uses SPECT brain-scanning to show the mechanisms by which negative thoughts, trauma, and even unforgiveness can physically damage the brain. With fresh focus, nutrition, forgiveness, and faith, the brain can be healed and optimized. He has made it possible for many to realize that mental illness is not a moral failure; it's most often an imbalance of the biology that grace and discipline can change.

Dr. Jeffrey Schwartz was a pioneer in bringing self-directed neuroplasticity to the mainstream – the belief that one can reshape their brain through repeated focus. His Four-Step Method helps people identify unhealthy thoughts, refocus on reality, and rewire their brain's response. He states, "The

---

[16] Mike Dow, *Healing the Broken Brain* (Hay House, 2017); Mike Dow, *The Brain Fog Fix* (Hay House LLC., 2016).

[17] Caroline Leaf, *Switch on Your Brain: The Key to Peak Happiness, Thinking, and Health* (Baker Books, 2013); Caroline Leaf, *Cleaning Up Your Mental Mess* (Baker Books, 2021).

[18] Daniel Amen, *Change Your Brain, Change Your Life* (Harmony, 2015); Daniel Amen, *Healing ADD* (Berkeley, 2013).

mind has the ability to change the brain. You are not your compulsions, your trauma, or your past. You are what you choose to focus on."[19] His Christian worldview supports the idea of biblical change through mental discipline and godly thinking.

These scientists show that **Romans 12:2** is not just a command – it is like a neuroscientific map of the brain. When you are renewing your mind with the Word of God, you are not just restoring your soul, you're reshaping your brain in real, verifiable, concrete ways.

You are not stuck in the darkness of your past. God has gifted you a very bright future. With His power, you can change your brain! Your God is faithful.

---

[19] Jeffrey Schwartz, *You Are Not Your Brain* (with Dr. Rebecca Gladding) (Avery, 2012).

Chapter 5: Recycling the Pain

Jesus had to be disfigured so that you can be transfigured –
Michael Williamson

"Consider it all joy, my brothers, when you meet trials of various kinds..." **(James 1:2 ESV)**

My wife and I have our own unique differences. There are fights over the thermostat that may trigger a second Vietnam War. There are disagreements over who must be taken into custody by the "Marriage Police" for the criminal offense of Cover Pulling – the abhorrent crime of yanking the covers at 3am. Somehow all of our relationship woes, the good and bad days, have been condensed and re-shaped (dare I say recycled?) into an online podcast entitled "The M&M Show." The show is part soap opera, part sitcom.[20]

However, the one thing that perfectly highlights our differences is the subject of recycling. My wife finds pure, almost spiritual joy in sorting plastics, bottles, and cardboard into little color-coded bins. To me, recycling feels like a

---

[20] I want to take this time to shout out the behind-the-scenes MVP'S Jessica, Franklin, Andrew Magno, Biancha, Patricia, and the rest of the crew for your tireless efforts! Michele and I know God's not done writing the script. Thank you for laughing with us, not at us!

guilt-powered pastime created by climate change activists who just needed another reason to shame strangers that hold plastic cups. Yet, even in this, I have had to (reluctantly at first and now joyfully) accept her enthusiasm.

I haven't become an eco-warrior (bring back the plastic straws I say!). I have come to appreciate her passion because I have realized something profound about the character of God. He is the ultimate recycler.

We recycle everything – paper, plastic, glass, and metal. We even recycle gossip, grudges, and Instagram reels. However, for many the concept of recycling our pain is off-limits. Instead we suppress it, numb it, and curse it. We blame God for the very thing He may be trying to use to make us great.

We typically look at a situation, think negatively, and see trash. But God sees triumph instead. He says, *"Consider it pure joy, my brothers and sisters, whenever you face trials of many kinds, because you know that the testing of your faith produces perseverance."* **(James 1:2-3)** We may see a young man abandoned by his father, but God sees a young man who will grow up to be a spiritual father to many. He also says, *"Though my father and mother forsake me, the Lord will receive me"* **(Psalm 27:10)** and *"Endure hardship as discipline; God is treating you as His children."* **(Hebrews 12:7)** Both Scriptures demonstrate in various ways that God's view of our circumstances radically differs from our own.

We see a woman scarred by sexual abuse, but God sees a powerful activist voice for the voiceless. He states, *"He will wipe every tear from their eyes. There will be no more death or mourning or crying or pain..."* **(Revelation 21:4)**

We see rubbish, but God smiles and labels it "restoration." A former porn addict becomes a passionate counsellor; a person serving a prison sentence can become a preacher. In man's view we see a huge trail of bad decisions, but God sees it as a riveting testimony under construction.

Psalm 30:11 states, *"You turned my wailing into dancing; you removed my sackcloth and clothed me with joy."*

The university drop-out can become a kingdom teacher in the making. Single mothers can give birth to the next world-changers. Malcolm X's mother Louise Little raised her children as a single mother after her husband died in what was claimed to be a streetcar accident and at one point was institutionalized. George Washington's mother, Mary Ball Washington, also raised her children alone after her husband died. Thomas Edison said this about his mother: "My mother was the making of me. She was so true, so sure of me; and I felt I had something to live for, someone I must not disappoint." God made this promise to women,

> *"Sing, barren woman, you who never bore a child; burst into song, shout for joy, you who were never in labor; because more are the children of the desolate woman than of her who has a husband,"* *says the Lord.* **(Isaiah 54:1)**

He also says, *she is clothed with strength and dignity; she can laugh at the days to come.* **(Proverbs 31:25)**

Few men shine brighter than Robert Smalls, one of my favorite heroes, as far as taking pain and recycling it into purpose. Born into slavery in 1839, Robert was not supposed to make history. He was supposed to be separated from his family, beaten for learning, mutilated for daring to think, and buried as a footnote in someone else's legacy.

Today, the world would be selling his pain to the media for clicks and likes, campaigning for his deification as the ultimate victim. That is the tragedy of our times; few want to hear the story of a black man who succeeds without bitterness or blame-shifting. Moreover, if they do, they assume it is because he was an entertainer or athlete.

But our God had a radically different plan. Robert Smalls did not just live through horrific pain, he recycled it, turning every scar into a strategy, every chain into courage, and every noose into a navigational point for destiny. His story doesn't pander to pity but calls us to purpose. He did not rise for revenge; instead, he rose for redemption.

In 1861, during the height of the bloodiest war in United States history,[21] the Civil War, Robert Smalls did the unthinkable. He stole a Confederate military ship, the *CSS Planter*, and disguised himself as the captain. With precision, courage, and brilliance, he used the Confederate

---

[21] The American Civil War claimed over 620,000 lives, more than 400,000 dying from disease like dysentery, typhoid, and pneumonia.

codebook, mastered the secret hand signals, passed multiple enemy checkpoints, and sailed his entire crew and their families – black men, women, and children – to freedom in the North.

Yet he didn't stop at freedom. He kept pushing forward, following principles of discipline, perseverance, persistence, and focus. He became a Union hero, recruiting over 5000 black soldiers to fight for liberty. He earned the rank of Captain, making him the highest-paid black soldier in US history. He also ran for US Congress and won.

Robert Smalls was a man who turned every one of his tears into triumph. He was a man who not only survived the horrors of slavery but overcame them without letting them define him. He turned injustice into national influence. His courage was not just about escape, but about empowerment. He transformed his tears into leadership, and his pain into political influence that set others free. Like Joseph, he probably would have agreed, *"What you meant for evil, God meant for good, to accomplish what is now being done, the saving of many lives."* **(Genesis 50:20)**

We get depressed because we have a failed marriage, but God sees powerful soil for deeper humility and healing with Him. He writes, *"Not only so, but we also glory in our sufferings, because we know that suffering produces perseverance; perseverance, character; and character, hope."* **(Romans 5:3-4)** He promises that *"The Lord is close to the brokenhearted and saves those who are crushed in spirit."* **(Psalm 34:18)**

Recycling isn't just about saving the planet, but about saving every broken piece of us and seeing it put to use. I never planned on learning profound lessons in a kitchen full of plastic bottles and cardboard, but watching my wife sort through them, I saw that God is a comedian. From Genesis to Revelation, He's taking lives that the world would label trash and recycling them into glorious testimonies. Jesus takes us, mess after mess, and recycles us into wonderful messages. Just look at their track record:

> Noah was a drunk … recycled into a builder of an ark of salvation.

> David was abandoned, overlooked, and an adulterer… recycled into a man after God's own heart.

> Jonah ran from God … but was recycled into a city-wide revival preacher.

> Paul was a murderer … recycled into a messenger of grace.

The cross was the ultimate recycling project ever created. The figure who appeared to be a waste – a man broken and nailed, bleeding from rejection – was turned into a well-spring of timeless salvation for every nation. God didn't throw away the cross; He used it to build the most revolutionary group of world-changing men in human history. He used the cross to save mankind.

Nor did Jesus just endure the cross – He transformed it. **Hebrews 12:2** states, *"For the joy set before Him, He endured the cross…"* Jesus didn't waste the betrayal, the lashes, the thorns, or the nails. He took the weapons of torture and turned them into the tools of triumph. He turned death into life, shame into glory, and graves into gateways. If Jesus recycled pain into purpose, so can we.

God doesn't just forgive us. He reuses us. He doesn't just throw our past aside; He recycles it into future potential and material for powerful preaching. Becoming a disciple of Jesus gives us so much more than the forgiveness of sins. It gives us a new life here on earth. The trash of our past is traded for the treasure of a purpose renewed by the grace of God.

We all have baggage, real baggage, heavy, ugly, stained baggage. We all come to God as if He was an airline employee, afraid that we will be kicked off the plane because of our oversized baggage that we have to take with us. Instead, He accepts everything and gives us a first-class seat.

We have hurt people, and we have been hurt. We have lived selfishly, acted in bitterness, fallen into lust, jealousy, rage, and impatience. We could probably fill a trash truck with the garbage of our past life. It is easy to cringe at the thought of Jesus lifting that lid and looking at everything. That is where Satan wants to have us – stuck playing what I call the shame-game, ashamed of our past, our weakness, ashamed to be completely open. We beg God to get rid of it all, but God doesn't erase our trash.

He re-uses it.

God does not just take out our trash; He recycles it into a trophy of grace. The pain you regret? Recycled into compassion. The failures you hate? Recycled into wisdom. The sins you can't shake? Recycled into testimonies that save other people. He redeems it to humble us. He redeems it to empower us. He redeems it to show a broken world what a redeemed life looks like.

> *Therefore, if anyone is in Christ, the new creation has come: The old has gone, the new is here!* **(2 Corinthians 5:17)**

Here are five men and women in the Bible who recycled their pain in powerful ways.

The first is Hagar. She was abused and abandoned, yet her life changed when she met "The God who sees." What we can learn from her is that the world may crush and discard us as nothing, but God still writes us into His story. We are highly valued to God and cannot let rejection define our value. We need to let God decide how we see the world and our situation. **(Genesis 16:13)** A way to do this is by writing a prayer journal entitled "The Lord Watches" or "God Sees Me." In it you can record moments when you meet God. Another way to do this is by creating a ministry in your church for single mothers who often feel unseen.

The second is Ruth. She was widowed and poor, a foreigner in Israel, but through her unshakeable loyalty to her mother-in-law, Naomi, she came to be listed in the bloodline of

Jesus. Like her, we can choose loyalty over comfort and look for opportunities to be exceptionally loyal. We can adopt a family or allow ourselves to be adopted by a family spiritually. **(Ruth 1:16-17)**

Then there is Hannah. She was barren and mocked, but her prayer and labor produced Samuel, a prophetic savior. Her pain produced a prophet. Your tears are not wasted. We can cry, pray, and keep moving. Sometimes, when God breaks us down, it is how we can have a breakthrough. **(1 Samuel 1:10-11)** To imitate Hannah, we can weep over and pray through past trauma, then make a clear decision to make one change in how we will respond in the present.

Another is Tamar. Her story is an interesting one, for she was silenced and shamed for tricking Judah, yet was held up as more righteous than he and honored in the Savior's lineage. Even when you have been wronged, God can recycle your pain. **(Genesis 38)** We can imitate Tamar by speaking our secrets aloud (with discernment). We can also start a podcast or write a book and share about our lives.

A famous example is Mary Magdalene. She had been delivered from seven demons by Jesus during His life and was the first witness to His resurrection. Your sin does not define you! No matter what our past, we can rise and tell the world about God, whether with others or alone. **(John 20:16-18)** We can also volunteer to help those suffering.

David, as mentioned earlier in the chapter, had many trials but learned to find strength in the Lord his God through each of them. **(1 Samuel 30:6)** When life burns everything we own down (physically or spiritually), worship is how we can rebuild ourselves before rebuilding others. Sometimes when things are falling apart, they are really falling into place. We need to find our strength not in human sympathy but in God. We can imitate David through writing songs, poems or looking for other artistic opportunities to recycle our suffering.

Paul was someone who faced many trials alone. In **2 Timothy 4:11** he writes *"Only Luke is with me..."* since all the others in his group had deserted him. Loneliness is a difficult cross to bear sometimes. However, just because you are standing alone does not mean you are standing on the wrong side. We need to stay the course, which we can do by writing material, producing books and content that will outlive our lives.

Another example is Joseph, who was criticized, hated, and betrayed because of his dream. Sometimes people will do the same to us. We need to decide that it doesn't matter if others can't see our dreams – it doesn't mean they didn't hear the dream. We need to protect our dream from critics and learn to be awesome and spiritual in moments where life seems unfair.

Ezekiel was someone who endured the grief of losing his beloved wife yet kept preaching God's word. **(Ezekiel 24:16-18)** Even when we suffer from a broken heart, it does not mean we have a broken calling. Pain is not a good reason to exit God's plan. Instead, we need to let loss move us to build the altar of surrender. We must serve when our heart gets broken and love when we are unappreciated.

Lastly, Jesus's example is one of keeping our hearts soft. He was betrayed by Judas and abandoned by all His disciples at the cross. However, betrayal by people is not betrayal by God. We need to stay God-focused and not man-focused. We need to decide not to let our past injuries harden our hearts. We can do that by making a vow to remain in our calling even when those closest to us betray us. We need to decide never to let man's weakness make us fall away.

Fortunately for me, our fellowship of churches is filled with disciples of Jesus who have recycled their pain. My own wife, Michele Williamson, was a survivor of horrific abuse, alcoholism, and despair, yet has built thriving churches globally, raised a faithful family with both children deciding to become baptized disciples, has a husband who absolutely adores her and encourages many disciples around the world. *"He gives beauty for ashes, the oil of joy for mourning."* **(Isaiah 61:3)**

Out of all the chapters in my life, one of the ones I hold most sacred is the one God is still writing in the life of my younger brother, Perry Williamson. I still remember the day he looked me in the eye and said, "Brother, despite the weaknesses in our mother… she taught us right from wrong. And the things I did as a young adult were wrong."

My heart stopped! His words hit me deep. You don't speak with that kind of honesty unless it comes from a deep cavern of suffering. That kind of statement comes from a soul that has been through a devastating urban war and decided to wave the flag of surrender... to God.

My younger brother is awesome! He didn't blame, spin, justify, or start running in the victim Olympics. He gathered himself, cleared his throat, and he owned it! When you're living in a world where you can download an excuse like the latest dating app, my younger brother showed poise. In this generation, where excuses are on clearance and accountability is rare, his words were miraculous.

He told me that if it weren't for God stepping in *after getting arrested, dodging multiple murder attempts,* and *facing death more times than he can count,* he doesn't know where he'd be. But I know. And so does he. He'd be another statistic. Another young black man behind a chalk outline. But grace intercepted him like a safety on 4th and goal! And today, my brother is grateful, God-fearing, and growing! I love you, Perry.

> *"You intended to harm me, but God intended it for good..."* **(Genesis 50:20)**

Perry is proof that survival is not success – but surrender is. My brother also proves that you can be surrounded by addiction, perversion, godless dysfunction, and generational trauma and still square your shoulders, sit up straight, and boldly declare: THIS STOPS WITH ME! Sadly, many in our family are still caught in a tornado of perversion, drugs, denial, and self-destruction. My lovely brother Perry has chosen to be a lighthouse, not driftwood.

I've seen street soldiers turn CEOs. I've seen ex-cons become examples. But what hits different is when it's your blood – your own brother – who turned tragedy into testimony.

> *The Lord is close to the brokenhearted and saves those who are crushed in spirit.* **(Psalm 34:18)**

So here's to you, Perry. You may not wear a collar or have a pulpit, but your life preaches louder than most sermons. You've been through hell and still chose heaven. You took some of the broken pieces of our family and built something special. I love you!

Cassidy Olmos, women's ministry leader for Barcelona, has been unable to have biological children though many avenues have been explored, but has raised countless spiritual sons and daughters around the world.

> *"Sing, barren woman ... you who were never in labor; because more are the children of the desolate woman..."* **(Isaiah 54:1)**

Ashley Tambaur, women's ministry leader for Stockholm, overcame the devastation of adultery. Her husband was unfaithful with another man, yet she chose faithfulness over bitterness, healing over hatred. Though she could have closed off her heart entirely, she remarried and now helps women in Sweden overcome the devastation caused by betrayal. Similarly, Hilarie Gordine faced heartbreak on the mission field from her first marriage. Though she fell away from God's church, she was restored, remarried, and now shepherds God's people with a beautiful family.

"I will restore you the years that the locusts have eaten…" **(Joel 2:25)**

Evangelist Blaise Feumba witnessed brutal atrocities during the civil war in Abidjan, yet he continues to serve as a powerful minister across Africa.

The light shines in the darkness, and the darkness has not overcome it. **(John 1:5)**

Bogdan, a leader in the Ukraine, stayed when the war broke out, despite bombs falling nightly and former leaders abandoning the people. He stays there still, defending and leading the people.

"Be strong and courageous. Do not be afraid… for the Lord your God goes with you." **(Deut. 31:6)**

Abhishek is a young man who came away from a near-death car crash when he was spiritually wandering and returned to God and was baptized. Later he baptized his mother and continues to serve the God's people around the world.

Wake up, sleeper, rise from the dead, and Christ will shine on you. **(Eph 5:14)**

Another young man also had a near-death experience. Lem's heart stopped due to an allergic reaction, but it led to his mother's spiritual heart starting, leading her to be baptized after his miraculous survival.

> *"This sickness will not end in death. No, it is for God's glory..."* **(John 11:4)**

Lastly Steph Thompson lived as a man for six years after chemically transitioning, but found God, de-transitioned back to being a woman, and is now a global voice of truth and healing and is dating a wonderful man of God.

> *Therefore, if anyone is in Christ, the new creation has come: The old has gone, the new is here!* **(2 Cor. 5:17)**

So, like my wife, I am now a proud recycler, at least when it comes to what truly matters. Maybe, just maybe, recycling isn't just about saving the planet but saving souls.

The Bible states that *"Those who sow in tears will reap with songs of joy."* **(Psalm 126:5)** Pain may be universal but its purpose is intentioned by God. You may not have stolen a ship, like Robert Smalls, but you can still steal back your destiny. Success is not only about doing great things and achieving a goal, but also about who you become in the process. It is for those who are willing to do what others will not and to have what others cannot.

Our suffering leads us to tears, but that is not the end of the story. Let what broke you build someone else. Let your injuries become inspirational to those out there still struggling. **2 Corinthians 1:4** states, *"He comforts us in all our troubles so that we can comfort those in any trouble with the comfort we ourselves receive from God."* Our transparency is someone else's transformation. Christian openness leads to more openness and more tears leads to more healing. **(1 John 1:5-10)**

Though pain can tempt us to throw ourselves a pity party, why not use it to fuel our mission instead! Nothing happens "to us;" everything happens "for us." God promises in **Romans 8:28** that *"And we know that in all things God works for the good of those who love Him..."* We can always ask: "How can this pain serve others?" and thereby flip our role from being a victim to being a vessel.

Leaders who recycle pain lead with humility, compassion, authority, vision, and boldness. Because they have survived fire and kept the faith, they have confidence, vision during suffering, and unwavering conviction. I learned in life that giving up is harder than trying and failing. Guilt will rot your soul worse than failure. Instead, we must be like those in **James 1:2-4**, *"Consider it pure joy ... whenever you face trials ... that you may be mature and complete, not lacking anything."*

Recycling pain is not about pretending the suffering did not happen. It is about letting God use, redeem, and multiply it into something influential.

Maybe the M&M show started as a side-splitting war between men and women, but in truth it is an example of the lives of my wife and I being recycled. Life, love, leadership – they are all about embracing the process of being broken, sorted, surrendered, and ultimately remade by a God who never throws away anything of value.

And trust me, He treasures your "garbage" more than you ever did.

Chapter 5: Recycling the Pain

Chapter 6: Tears of Betrayal

If an enemy were insulting me, I could endure it;
If a foe were rising against me, I could hide.
But it is you, a man like myself, my companion, my close friend,
With whom I once enjoyed sweet fellowship at the house of God,
As we walked about among the worshipers. **(Psalm 55:12-14)**

What is friendly fire? Historically, this term was popularized in World War 2 and the Vietnam War. In essence, friendly fire is the accidental attack from soldiers who are fighting on the same side. These wounds are inflicted not by the enemy but by fellow soldiers and allies. An example was in 1991 when US forces mistakenly shot down their own aircraft. Public outrage flooded the media at the time and global attention skyrocketed! In the Gulf War, 35 of the 148 American combat deaths were due to friendly fire, making up about 23% of the total US battle fatalities. Similarly, the Los Angeles Times highlighted that friendly fire incidents resulted in the deaths of nine British soldiers and injuries to 13 others. Although "friendly" is more palatable a term, the fire is unexpected, disheartening, and lethal.

In God's Kingdom, friendly fire is all too real. I've been on the receiving side many times. It is an attack from within the ranks of the church, from those who were meant to fight beside you. The battle turns brutal when betrayal takes the form of backroom conversation cloaked as "concern," or when gossip dresses itself up in false humility. Sometimes it comes as a theological opinion subtly weaponized to undermine authority. Other times, it is envy that sharpens itself into godless character assassination. And then there's the most painful shot of all: spiritual abandonment by those you once called family to the end. These are a shot to the heart, breaking the skin, for no one has the power to hurt you like your friends.

Friendly fire wounds deeply because it comes from friendly hands – and that's what makes the tears harder to dry. The danger lies in it being unexpected, intimate, shaking your faith, and causing spiritual internal bleeding. Of course, God allows friendly fire to refine us, not destroy us.

Let us not forget the great lessons learned by David.

> *His talk is smooth as butter, yet war is in his heart.*
> **(Psalm 55:21)**

David was sharp, but friendly fire sharpened him even more. He learned that not every soft voice comes from a spiritually safe heart. His betrayal taught him to look beyond charisma, to character, beyond words, to the spirit. Friendly fire gave him dynamic discernment.

Betrayal helps us learn to love without being naive! David grew in wisdom, but he was not gullible. Yes, he was a man who led from the heart but with eyes wide open.

But as for me, I trust in you. **(Psalm 55:23)**

Wow, Psalm 55 recounts David being betrayed by his most trusted counselor, Ahithophel, who tried to split the church with Absalom. This is dangerous because Ahithophel weaponized his wisdom when David was vulnerable. The poetic irony is that Ahithophel's name means "foolish brother." I guess his name teaches us even the loyal and wise can become fools. Sometimes the most gifted can become dangerous when the heart drifts from God as Ahithophel took his own life. Yet David says, I trust in you. I can hear the "Old Testament Mic" dropping at this point.

David learned that the main focus is to remain focused! David didn't waste his energy on slander, revenge, meaningless competition, or getting even; he got better. The Psalms highlight that he developed a deeper trust in God.

Perhaps the blade of friendly fire has stabbed you in the back. Those who move forward prove allegiance was always to God first, not people. David was deeply hurt by friendly fire, but it sharpened his trust, deepened his wisdom, and matured his heart. It also gave him one of the most emotive, worshipful, and honest prayer lives in the Bible. The same can be true for you and me!

The church will inevitably experience "friendly fire" because it contains members who hail from various ethnic backgrounds and socially disparate circumstances who possess sinful human characteristics. The church should exist within the world, but the world should not contaminate the church. Unfortunately, some of the worst wounds can happen "behind church walls." That spiritual manipulation, broken relationships, and sexual abuse can dismantle the trust in a place meant to be a haven may be surprising but not uncommon. Leaders do misuse their authority. Members crucify leaders with their grumbling, fault-finding, and self-righteous virtue signalling.

The hurt from being wounded by a brother or sister strikes deeper than any other. Betrayal becomes worse when the betrayer was once your prayer partner or someone who introduced you to Christianity. The agony of friendly fire occurs when those who shared ministry duties with you become the source of your burns. The sting from someone who walks beside you in faith creates a sharp and intense pain. While these are three of the most excruciating stings known to man: the bullet ant, which delivers agony up to 24 hours; the tarantula hawk, which causes instantaneous lightning-like pain; and the executioner wasp, which produces a sting that remains painful for days – the greatest sting is described in the Bible!

> *The sting of death is sin, and the power of sin is the law. But thanks be to God! He gives us victory through our Lord Jesus Christ!* **(1 Corinthians 15:56-57)**

While insect stings torment the physical body, sin stings the body of Christ – and without Jesus, the pain is eternal for those outside Christ.

When leaders fall, mentors fail, and movements divide, the foundation of your faith is severely tested. It is in these times that the temptation to protect your heart and extinguish your tears may be the greatest. Loyalty makes betrayal more tragic. In the Bible, Uriah the Hittite was loyal to his wife, Bathsheba; to his king, David; and to his military commander, Joab, but all three betrayed him. He was the kind of man who would not sleep with his wife while his fellow soldiers were in battle. He was more committed while drunk than David was sober. Yet sometimes, even noble loyalty can be unwise. Uriah's unwavering devotion to the war made him blind to the battle within his military outpost. He sadly trusted the orders of Joab, the kind of man who would follow a wicked command even if it reeked of betrayal. Uriah carried his own death warrant unknowingly, hand-delivered it to the man who would orchestrate his execution. Joab, the ever-loyal, cold-hearted strategist with no moral compass, obeyed an evil order, making him an accomplice in armor. **(2 Samuel 11)**

There is a danger in being more committed to the mission than to the truth. Uriah's fate teaches us that loyalty, when weaponized by the corrupt, can be fatal. He was killed by the system he served, not because of weakness but because of righteous obedience. Ironically, Uriah's life might have been spared if he had trusted the bad-hearted David. If he had gone home, if he had abandoned his loyalty to the battle just long enough to follow the manipulative plan, he would have lived. However, Uriah was too righteous to suspect unrighteousness, too loyal and good-hearted to assume betrayal was an option.

Uriah's integrity cost him his life, but it may have saved David's! In a strange twist, obedience without discerning flawed leadership is what led to his death. Sometimes the most tragic deaths come not from failure, but from faithfulness in the wrong hands. There will always be men like Joab, a military commander who won every fight but without the right heart. Joab stood beside David in battle, but not in spirit. He was loyal only to the victories in the Kingdom, not the vision of truly changing the world with the love of God. Joab's life teaches us that not all success is an indication of sincerity. His sword defended the kingdom but never feared the King. **(1 Chron. 11:6; 2 Samuel 3:39)** Joab's loyalty was only for the long game of personal gain. His eventual execution wasn't due to poetic justice – it was the consequence of an unchecked heart and untested loyalty.

History repeats this pattern. Just as David had Joab, America had Benedict Arnold – once a trusted general, later a cowardly traitor. I can imagine the eyes of William Wallace (protagonist in the movie *Braveheart)* being like those of Uriah, looking straight into the eyes that betrayed him with a single tear when he realized the sinister truth. This might be the same penetrating gaze Jesus gave Judas Iscariot in the Garden. Both history and Biblical stories show the same thing. This would have been the gaze Julius Caesar had when his right-hand man, Brutus, drove the knife in to kill him, with the same shock that Samson's eyes would have had when Delilah's deception destroyed his destiny. Joseph must have felt the same silent pain, shedding tears from the abandonment by his brothers. Or perhaps the same expression was in the eyes of Leonidas at Thermopylae, outnumbered, betrayed, yet dying with a general's honor.

Every leader betrayed by a fellow brother or sister knows sometimes the most significant battles are not fought on the battlefield but through the tears shed over the quiet aftermath of friendly fire.

Three years after becoming a sold-out disciple, I met the love of my life, the beautiful Michele Williamson. This may sound cliché, but it was love at first sight. We locked eyes across a packed arena, and I heard what I believed was the voice of God say, "She's the one, Michael, yes, her, she's the one."

Seeing my wife for the first time completely took me off my guard. I usually recognize beauty and appreciate it without being shaken too much, admiring it, appreciating it, and moving on as if it were no big deal. Not so with Michele. There was something about her that I could not quite place, something deeply intriguing, spiritually captivating, and classy. She was not just beautiful – she was unforgettable.

We got married two years later. I cannot describe the tingling sensation of purity, love, joy, and euphoria; it was life changing. Given the visa deadline of eleven quick days, Michele and I were married in a lovely home in Beaverton,

Oregon. To be joined in marriage by the very man who led me to Christ was special. I still remember it clearly – a deep spiritual calm seemed to rest on us, like heaven shined a spotlight, not on the stage like those I was used to, but on two vulnerable hearts making a covenant. I can remember it as a sacred pause in time like the silence in heaven. There was no loud applause from people, just approval from God. We were both principal actors in the Lord's redemptive story, and I felt like God leaned in and whispered in my ear, *"Well done, my good and faithful servant(s)."* **(Matthew 25:23)**

The day we were married was incredibly sunny, once again reminding me of some of the most significant life-changing days of my life. I had finally done it – I was en route to accomplishing one of my most precious dreams: a family. We had dated purely for an entire year, not so much as holding hands. Michele's hands were too soft and beautiful for me to hold without serious temptation.

We remained pure for six more days before our formal wedding in the church. As a concession, after the legal marriage we decided to hold hands, though it became a little intense. But we made it, by God's grace.

Our honeymoon was one of the best times of my life. It was full of joy, happiness, and peace. We joked with each other, laughing until 1 am on several nights.

There was a power and confidence that came over me when I introduced Michele not as my girlfriend but as my wife. We were just at a corner store, and I casually mentioned it to the clerk. He barely looked up and gave me a kind of half-smile, "Cool story, bro…" like it meant nothing. But to me it meant everything. Saying it out loud made it real. It wasn't a movie set and there was no camera crew. This wasn't the set of *Men of Honor* where I had a small speaking part. This time I wasn't acting like a man of honor for the cameras. I was one.

In my mind I had stepped into the responsible category of people. I still remember looking into Michele's eyes taking photos of her as we made snow angels in the sand at Cannon Beach. We had no money or fancy cars, but we had God and now we had each other.

A few days later, returning to the church that had married us was like running through a Portland blizzard without a shirt. The church felt like a home where people had already moved out, with empty smiles, packed bags, cold stares, and frozen hearts. A single bitter letter, written by a former members fueled by resentment, anger, half-truths, and contempt tore through the congregation like wildfire while we were gone. In days we went from 300 members to barely 75.

It felt like abandonment all over again. Flashbacks of being left in that crack house as a child flooded my mind – my mother gone, the loneliness thick, the pain fresh again. I was married, but I felt orphaned because the pressure of everyone leaving put a strain on my young marriage. Michele and I were divided almost as soon as we were united, because we stood on opposing sides of the issues raised in the church.

My secret weapon was always my prayer life, but the sadness that came over me was like carrying a dead bear. For the first time in my life, I felt the weight of depression worse than the abandonment. "I'm gonna lose my wife ... my church ... and my mind," I thought. I was so deeply gray, sad, frustrated, and confused I couldn't even pray. I lost my appetite, fielding several calls from bitter disciples criticizing my stance on righteousness over rebellion. I felt like I was watching our church building go up in flames, then being blamed for holding a firehose. I didn't expect any applause for protecting the church into which I had poured my life, but I also didn't expect vitriol and backlash. I heard it all: "You're too harsh, you're too happy, you're too young, you're too hopeful."

The negative feedback and criticism cut me deep, not because it was loud, but because I came from those I loved. Sadly, many of these members taught me key scriptures they sinfully decided not to obey. Some were heroes who had inspired me. Each day, when I returned home to check my voicemail, there was a flurry of negative messages criticizing me. One sister said "Michael, you will never be successful in ministry." I don't know why, but that was the last of roughly ten messages – and like a flaming arrow, somehow it got through and hit my heart.

Instantly I plummeted into a darkness I can't really explain in words. My chest caved under the weight of the moment. I collapsed on the kitchen floor and cried. Many who left the church were former leaders, espousing their bitter views of the kingdom to any willing ear. I am reminded of the Jews condemned in Scripture with millstones tied around their necks for leading others astray. **(Luke 17:2)** Sadly, the letter that started the entire division gave people who wanted to leave the excuse they were looking for. It also highlighted glaring sins and obvious mistakes we made building the churches. I was heartbroken again. I thought the kingdom would be the answer to all my fears of abandonment. Sadly, I was abandoned again. Why me, God?

To make things worse, this tragic church split happened 30 days after I watched my mother convulse, taking her last breath. For two weeks, I had tried studying the Bible with her, holding out hope she could make it at the very end, but she died in the living room of her small, cold apartment. I can still recall the scent of oxygen tanks, cigarettes, medical gauze, and aging carpet. The scene was filled with chaotic screaming and physical family members that were so hurt they loaded their guns and headed to the streets. The disciples who came to help me that night were visibly shaken and left me there. I was so disoriented by her death that I didn't leave until the next day.

Now this. The church was supposed to be my sanctuary from the chaos of my mother. Now it felt like my church was dying, my young marriage was dying, and so was I. The timing of all this felt unbearable and cruel. I had thoughts like, "Do I still need to smile, lead, and pretend everything is ok? Maybe I should just quit myself?" My soul was bleeding from personal tragedy, and my church was bleeding from friendly fire.

I now realize that in life, suffering never checks your calendar or schedules the best day.

However, I had fought too hard to become a Christian, so quitting was not an option. Without leaders to get advice from, without mother or father to call, and without a wife to confide in as she was hurt herself, I found I couldn't even pray. I tried, but nothing would come out.

Except for a song: "O Lord, prepare me to be a sanctuary…"

I sang it over and over again, sometimes whispering it through tears, sometimes just breathing it. That melody became my survival. It was all I had.

And for the first time, I understood what I was asking – that God prepare not a building, not a crowd of people, but me to be a sanctuary, to carry God's presence when the temple crumbles, to be the sacred place in the chaos when God gives me the most difficult challenges. "Pure and holy, tried and true … with (ahem)…. Thanksgiving, I'll be a living sanctuary for you!"

I sang my way through the suffering. I held on to the melody of that song as my tears became more powerful than every sermon I remembered. I have found that throughout history courageous individuals confronted their mission's challenges by using their voices and music to overcome waves of discouragement.

The Titanic's band performed "Nearer My God to Thee" during the boat's sinking in 1912, which transformed the passengers' fear of death into immediate courage. Jewish prisoners sang "Hatikvah" before their execution in Nazi camps because it represented their enduring faith and hope despite their impeding death. American slaves performed spirituals like "Swing Low, Sweet Chariot" in cotton fields to worship and plan escape routes through their music. Martin Luther King, Jr., led the Civil Rights Movement through "We Shall Overcome," using melody as resistance during beatings, rapes, imprisonments, and Satanic lynchings. The loss of his four daughters at sea inspired Horatio Spafford to write "It Is Well With My Soul," and his hymn provided widespread healing. Dietrich Bonhoffer performed hymns during his final hours in a Nazi prison, which shocked the prison guard because of his peaceful, humble, faithful demeanor. Even now, as missiles fall from the sky in the Ukraine, families take shelter in the subway stations and sing, "How Great Thou Art."

All of these people imitate Paul and Silas, who sang, as it says in **Acts 16:25-6**: *"About midnight Paul and Silas were praying and singing hymns to God… and suddenly there was a violent earthquake…"*

Like Paul the apostle, singing set me free in the prison of my suffering. God wasn't rebuilding the old temple; He was tearing it down. He was rebuilding me.

And that was the real miracle.

One of the temptations during suffering through friendly fire is to become sentimental and value the relationship over righteousness. **Numbers 16** records how Korah, a Levite, rebelled not out of doctrinal concern, but out of discontent with his role. He persuaded 250 men of renown to follow him. Pelah withdrew and saved his own soul by not joining the faction. Sentimentality toward sin is more dangerous than rebellion itself. When we mourn the wrong things, we share in judgement.

Korah's descendants, however, chose righteousness. They became powerful, inspiring, and deeply influential as some of the greatest worship leaders in the Bible, writing Psalms like **Psalm 42** and **84**. **Psalm 42:1** exclaims, *"As the deer pants for streams of water, so my soul pants for you, my God."*

An example of someone who survived all kinds of fire was the Apostle John. He endured religious persecution, the betrayal of Jesus by Judas, abandonment by his own church family, and multiple Roman emperors and their attempts to kill him. He survived verbal rejection **(3 John 9-10)**, religious opposition **(Acts 4:19-21)**, terror from Nero, and Domitian exiling him to Patmos. He saw Domitian dip Christians in blood to mock baptisms, throwing them to wild dogs. Disciples were burned alive to offer lights to the Roman streets. Families were dismantled, homes confiscated, anyone who claimed Jesus as Lord could die on the spot. John shed endless tears watching his friends tortured. Can you imagine the emotional trauma from seeing all this?

Even though the book of Revelations was birthed through brutality, it is a book that declares victory, showcasing John's faithfulness despite trials. During what seemed like hell he still shed tears of victory!

Revelation 2:7: *"To the one who is victorious, I will give the right to eat form the tree of life, which is the paradise of God."*

Revelation 2:11: *"The one who is victorious will not be hurt at all by the second death."*

Revelation 2:17: *"To the one who is victorious, I will give some of the hidden manna. I will also give that person a white stone with a new name written on it, known only to the one who receives it."*

Revelation 2:26: *"To the one who is victorious and does my will to the end, I will give authority over the nations."*

Revelation 3:5: *"The one who is victorious will, like them, be dressed in white. I will never blot out the name of that person from the book of life, but will acknowledge that name before my Father and His angels."*

Revelation 3:12: *"The one who is victorious I will make a pillar in the temple of my God. Never again will they leave it...."*

Revelation 3:21: *"To the one who is victorious, I will give the right to sit with me on my throne, just as I was victorious and sat down with my Father on His throne."*

John's secret was survival. He stayed faithful through friendly fire, religious fire, and imperial fire. He survived. He was victorious!

Winston Churchill experienced deep emotional pain and complexity in his relationship with his father, Lord Randolph Churchill. Lord Randolph maintained a critical stance towards young Winston while remaining emotionally distant and dismissive. Even though Lord Randolph achieved political prominence, he lacked trust in his son's capabilities. Through correspondence, he repeatedly demeaned Winston by labelling him a letdown and threatening to become "a mere social wastrel" unless he showed improvement. Churchill developed an unyielding determination to demonstrate his worth. He recycled the suffering into a motivational force, which helped him achieve victory in World War II.

The early church experienced difficulties because of its swift expansion. **(Acts 6)** The combination of honesty, grace, and truth along with self-awareness and humility can effectively heal many wounds. Conflict that is addressed with righteousness strengthens family bonds and deepens relationships by functioning much like iron that sharpens iron. **(Prov. 27:17)**

We need to decide not to let disloyalty reassign our place on the battlefield, even if the voice that once guided us now echoes in deceit. We cannot allow bitterness to become our identity, as we've been betrayed but not completely broken. We may have been cut by the hand that held ours in prayer, but God's healing hand always stretches the furthest.

Jesus is our example of how to manage unexpected betrayal. Betrayed by a kiss by Judas, abandoned by His disciples, mocked by the crowds He healed, while hanging on a cross He said, *"Father, forgive them, for they know not what they do."* **(Luke 23:34)**

Forgiveness is the only answer.

Here are some practical steps to surviving spiritual betrayal:

1) Mourn with discernment: We need to feel the pain but not follow the fall or the fallen. We need to continue following the word of God.
2) Cling to Your Calling: Emotions change, but your calling does not. We need to forgive and embrace our calling more than ever. We were called for such a time as this.
3) Recycle the suffering into a song and sermon: We need to continue studying the Bible intensely. We can learn lessons about God through any trial.
4) Anchor in Scripture, not sentiment: We need to let the word of God define our loyalty, not our emotions, injuries, leadership position, or opinions.

5) Trust God's faithfulness and forgive: Even if man fails you, God never will. We need to forgive others as Christ forgave us. Forgiveness is unlocking the door to set a person free, only to realize the prisoner was you.

C.S. Lewis said, "To be a Christian means to forgive the inexcusable because God has forgiven the inexcusable in you."

When Satan tries to shatter your heart in pieces, it is important to remember that you can get a better heart from a broken heart. The Japanese have a process of repairing broken pottery called Kintsugi. This is an art form that does not hide the cracks in pottery but highlights them and fills them with gold to make the broken pottery stronger. Similarly, God can fill those broken places with a faith that is as good as gold.

Scars become stories. Pain becomes power.

Chapter 7: Tears of Compassion

"During the days of Jesus' life on earth, He offered up prayers and petitions with fervent cries and tears." **(Hebrews 5:7)**

"The truth is everybody is going to hurt you: you just gotta find the ones worth suffering for." ~Bob Marley

Soon afterward, Jesus went to a town called Nain, and His disciples and a large crowd went along with Him. As He approached the town gate, a dead person was being carried out–the only son of his mother, and she was a widow. And a large crowd from the town was with her. When the Lord saw her, His heart went out to her and He said, "Don't cry."

Then He went up and touched the bier they were carrying him on, and the bearers stood still. He said, "Young man, I say to you, get up!" The dead man sat up and began to talk, and Jesus gave him back to his mother.

They were all filled with awe and praised God. "A great prophet has appeared among us," they said. "God has come to help His people." This news about

145

Chapter 7: Tears of Compassion

Jesus spread throughout Judea and the surrounding country. **(Luke 7:11-17)**

This story depicts a heartbroken mother preparing to bury her only child, her sole source of hope. I can imagine her slow walk to the graveyard as she carries her only hope in her arms. This would represent a time of realization, "I am getting ready to bury my legacy, my livelihood."

This widow was not walking or talking to God. She wasn't even looking for Jesus amid this hopeless situation. She had no husband to provide financial security and now no son to offer protective security, and no one else to lean on.

Yet she just so happens to meet Jesus. He had travelled to the town of Nain with His disciples and a large crowd in tow. The town's inhabitants were forming a large crowd around the woman.

The Bible says, *"His heart went out to her."* The Greek word for compassion here is *splagchnizomai*, meaning "from the gut" or "from the bowels." Ancients believed the deepest emotions came from the gut. It shows that Jesus did not just feel sympathy in a superficial way; His entire being was moved. He had a "gut feeling" and did not emotionally detach from the situation. Touching the coffin, as Jesus did, would have made Him ceremonially unclean, but He did it anyway. He touched those considered untouchable. For Jesus, having compassion meant crossing boundaries, touching the pain, and then giving hope.

The people in town had the strength to carry the dead body, but not to resurrect him. As great as that is, we need to go beyond and be like Jesus and give hope in hurting situations.

I am eternally grateful for the men and women God sent into my life, who saw through my pride and insecurity while on my funeral walk in the world. The Portland Church of Christ studied the Bible with me seven different times for over 16 months before I finally decided to be baptized. Paul Williams called me every week for a year, despite my never answering. Barbara Duval provided encouragement, saying, "You can do it, Michael." Scott Lunde's radical example shook my excuses, Jeremy Ciaramella's wisdom, humility, and precisions with the Scriptures changed my life. Later, Kian Nikzi reached out to the woman of my dreams. Others included Matt Kennedy, Jason Andrew, and Jacob Beas. Christian Lacava studied with my mother and taught me to forgive my past. Tony and Therese Untalan rallied the church to give financially so I could bury my mother.

Then there was Paul Grover, who not only challenged me to dive deeper into the Word of God but also taught me the meaning of true family. He served me in quiet, powerful ways, opening his heart and home, and even later providing me the space where my wife and I could celebrate our honeymoon. I can also remember Bob, who had been a part of the Aryan Brotherhood and skinhead movement in Oregon, who had been hardened by hate but was now humbled by Jesus. He was one of the first men to study the Bible with me, a black man. Tears of love and compassion can rewrite a legacy.

The gospel of the cross doesn't just save souls and forgive sin, it leads us to a level of compassion that shatters the walls of racism and hate and makes family out of enemies.

The Apostle Paul's humility and compassion stand in strong contrast with many others, both now and even in the Bible. Paul was so impacted by the grace of God that it inspired him to work harder than all the other apostles, saying in **1 Corinthians 15:10**: *"But by the grace of God I am what I am, and His grace to me was not without effect. No, I worked harder than all of them—yet not I, but the grace of God that was with me."* His humility, insight, perseverance, and resilience were forged in the fire of suffering, pain, disappointment, and difficult times. God had said before his baptism, *"I will show him how much he must suffer for my name."* **(Acts 9:16)** It was undoubtedly the genuine understanding that he persecuted Christians that compelled him to empathize with hurting Jews and Gentiles alike. Paul was powerful because he learned that pain had a purpose.

Paul expressed this in **1 Corinthians 9:19-23**:

> *Though I am free and belong to no one, I have made myself a slave to everyone, to win as many as possible. To the Jews I became like a jew, to win the Jews. To those under the law I became like one under the law (though I myself am not under the law), so as to win those under the law. To those not having the law I became like one not having the law (though I am not free from God's law but am under Christ's law), so as to win those not having the law. To the*

weak I became weak, to win the weak. I have become all things to all people so that by all possible means I might save some. I do all this for the sake of the gospel, that I may share in its blessings.

For Paul, the priority was selflessly putting seeking and saving the lost as a higher priority than his own life. As he says in **Romans 9:3**, *"For I could wish that I myself were cursed and cut off from Christ for the sake of my people, those of my own race…"*

His humility is also seen in **2 Corinthians 11:16-33**. Here Paul boasts not in the triumphs he has experienced, but rather in his sufferings, saying in verse 30, *"If I must boast, I will boast of the things that show my weakness."*

After we shed tears of loss, tears of truth, tears shed in the darkness, and even tears of betrayal, the tears will start to dry, and that is when we can start taking our eyes off ourselves. We will have gained the faith to be outward focused, and our tears will become tears of compassion shed for the lost. We will have learned to change our minds about our suffering and see the purpose in our pain. We will have learned the lessons of gaining a security deeply rooted in the unshakable love of God, which allows us to be vulnerable, honest, and effective in helping other hurting souls.

Part of the journey is through prayer. Prayer doesn't just change the situation; it changes the person praying. In my first year as a disciple, I shed more tears in prayer than I ever had before – for my mother, for my brothers, for lost souls.

At times I felt embarrassed that the only way I knew how to connect with God deeply was through praying about these wounds.

Over time, I realized, prayer doesn't change God. Prayer changes you.

Psalm 6:6-9 says, *"I am worn out from my groaning. All night long I flood my bed with weeping and drench my couch with tears ... The Lord has heard my cry for mercy; the Lord accepts my prayer..."* God did not change the situation for David; He changed his soul. Each tear shed brought him closer to God, who absolutely was listening. **Psalm 34:17-18** says, *"The righteous cry out, and the Lord hears them; He delivers them from all their troubles. The Lord is close to the brokenhearted and saves those who are crushed in spirit."* When we get distracted by trouble, prayer brings us back to God, not because he is far but because we have been wandering. Prayer does not always deliver you from trouble, but it delivers you through trouble."

Psalm 42:3-5 is hilarious: *"My tears have been my food day and night... Why, my soul, are you downcast? ... Put your hope in God."* The Psalmist started off by talking about his tears to God and ends up preaching to himself. This has happened to me so many times. Prayers and tears lead you through the night to the joy of the morning. This is not because God changes anything, but because we do: *"Weeping may tarry for the night, but joy comes with the morning."* **(Psalm 30:5 ESV)**

Each tear I shed in prayer was not wasted. Every tear that ran down my face, although unanswered in the way I expected, was heard by the God who is outside time, space, and matter – the God who sees the end from the beginning. Even though my family did not change, friends did not change, situations did not change, strangely enough, I did. God was recycling my pain into perseverance, shifting my focus from results to reverence. God was training me to value intimacy over outcome. My prayer life changed from a consistent disappointment because of unanswered requests, to consistent conversations because of an undeniably close relationship.

Leonard Ravenhill said, "The self-sufficient do not pray, the self-satisfied will not pray, the self-righteous cannot pray." Corrie Ten Boom said, "God never sends us into a storm without first teaching us how to pray in the rain."

We live in a generation obsessed with running the "victim Olympics." We see outrage flooding every corner of the internet, with people sharing why it is someone else's fault that they are hurting. Few people honestly take personal responsibility for where their lives are at and learn how to surrender their suffering to God. Without God, tears dry into bitterness instead of beauty.

Aleksandr Solzhenitsyn, who won a Nobel Peace Prize for his writings about how he survived the Soviet labor camps, said something that sadly describes the 21st century: "Men have forgotten God; that's why all this has happened." He wasn't merely commenting on political collapse or human cruelty; he was pointing to the wickedness and cruelty of the human heart that has no reverence for God. Without God, we have no true reason to be compassionate. The absence of God causes compassion to dry up alongside our tears. Instead of our tears becoming pools of healing, they freeze and become bridges to bitterness. When we let our tears dry up without God's influence, they harden our hearts.

However, when we allow tears to dry with the help of Jesus, we allow hope to interrupt our funeral procession. It is at this time that tears heal our hearts.

The healing process has no actual finish line, but the fruits are abundant enough to evangelize the nations in one generation. Drying tears do not mean we are done grieving. They mean we are starting to breathe again, to believe again. They mean we are no longer hiding from our wounds but facing them. Tears are not the end of the story. They are how the heart begins to write its next chapter.

The sign of true healing is when we mature into shedding tears of compassion. We will then weep with those who weep, without being crushed in spirit ourselves. We will rejoice with those who rejoice, without being envious.

The day I was baptized, the two visitors who came with me weren't celebrities or even family – they were two homeless campus students I had met just hours before. After inviting countless friends to my baptism and hearing silence, I drove around looking for someone with whom to share my joy. I had spotted these two begging for money. At first, I debated giving them ten dollars, then twenty or thirty.

Finally, I approached them and blurted out, "You guys – want to go to dinner with me?" They looked stunned, as if unsure whether to trust me. Five minutes later, they were in my car, riding to the nicest steakhouse I could find. We talked for hours. I spoke with such uncontainable joy about getting baptized that I probably freaked them out. That night, they stayed at my house, and the next day they came to church with me.

The girl confided in me that she had been using crack and living in a crack house. After church, they showed me where they lived. It wasn't just poverty – it was total depravity and devastation. It was surreal. I knew exactly what was happening inside that house without entering. Memories flooded back: seeing people come in and out of my childhood home, searching other crack houses for my mother.

Strangely, I wasn't shocked. I gave them advice as if I had been living with them all along. I tried to study the Bible with them, but they were not open to hearing about the gospel. I searched for them for weeks afterwards, even when I was warned it was too dangerous to go back into the area.

I didn't care. I had tasted the compassion of Christ, and I burned to share it. I had broken through with God in prayer, and I felt like His angel to avenge a hurting world.

Chapter 7: Tears of Compassion

In addition to the suffering my upbringing brought into my life, I have been in some harrowing situations building the church. Thus far, the most extreme case was being able to help a man who was having sex with dead bodies to become a disciple of Jesus. I have helped pedophiles and prostitutes in Portland and a serial rapist in California. I have discipled many with HIV and hepatitis, studied with a convicted killer from Chicago, and an international drug lord. I converted a Satanist here in London whose sin list was so debased it scared me to listen to him read it. I have worked with the rich, the intellectually complicated, and those who were jarringly destitute. Some have not become or remained faithful to God, including a hurting single mother, a woman we all loved, who refused to heed discipling, fell away from God, became pregnant, and tragically lost her life giving birth.

I have also seen close friends abandon their faith and watched spiritual sons, men I called brothers, turn into my greatest opponents. Much like Winston Churchill, whose fiercest critic was his own father, I have known the grief of spiritual disownment. Men I deeply respected, leaders I once followed, sent me back to the very place of abandonment.

And yet, I still say it: having a life rich in suffering is a blessing. Because it is in suffering that pride is stripped away, faith is forged, and compassion becomes more than just a word – it becomes a way of life.

When we protect others from the trauma of life, we also prevent them from strengthening their emotions to the point of compassion. We can put people on a path that leads to great disappointment, frustration, and emotional weakness by trying to protect them from every pain in life. There is no virtue in victimization, but there is also no character without a softened heart. We need to be able to say, like the Psalmist does, *"Though my father and mother forsake me, the Lord will receive me,"* **(Psalm 27:10)** and *"We are hard pressed on every side, but not crushed; perplexed, but not in despair…"* **(2 Corinthians 4:8)**

Real tears of compassion do not reveal sentimental weakness but resilient power glorifying God through a selfless heart of tenderness and empathy. Our brother Paul was hard pressed but not crushed, and we too can let suffering deepen our conviction, as opposed to being damaged by its affliction. Compassion compelled Jesus to do so much, and it should compel you. **(2 Corinthians 5:14)** He healed out of compassion, **(Mathew 14: 14)** preached out of compassion, **(Mark 6:34)** shared out of compassion, **(Mathew 15:32)** and in the end, he died because of his compassion. **(Romans 5:8)** May your tears of compassion first compel your heart to feel, **(Romans 12: 15)** to pray, **(Mathew 9:36-38)** then to act out of compassion for a hurting world. **(1 John 3:17-18)** Perhaps this book will help change your perspective to develop the mental fortitude to love yourself and others. This love comes not despite suffering but because you let it "make you," not "break you."

Chapter 7: Tears of Compassion

Chapter 8: Tears of Laughter and Joy

Tears of Joy

Therefore, since we are surrounded by such a great cloud of witnesses, let us throw off everything that hinders and the sin that so easily entangles. And let us run with perseverance the race marked out for us, fixing our eyes on Jesus, the pioneer and perfecter of faith. For the joy set before Him He endured the cross, scorning its shame, and sat down at the right hand of the throne of God. Consider Him who endured such opposition from sinners, so that you will not grow weary and lose heart. **(Hebrews 12:1-3)**

A woman entering into pregnancy understands the purpose of the pains of childbirth. Her newfound happiness and maternal bliss do not wipe away all the tears, but she understands the end goal. When everything is all said and done, she will be looking at her little bundle of joy. An athlete endures painful hours of training because he understands the purpose. Every time we are inspired to run further, push harder, or lift heavier, we are exposing ourselves to pain. Some athletes will go so far as to play through an apparent injury because of the power of a motivating purpose. The student understands that academic pressure associated with achieving a doctorate is par for the course. The lonely nights, and in some cases depression, is

157

acceptable because they know the purpose of the academic degree they are achieving. The suffering is worth it, and the joy of making it through is doubly worth it. We can go as far as paying for pain as long as it is part of the purpose. Tattoo parlors, personal trainers, Hollywood surgeons all understand this concept and profit handsomely from it.

We only hate pain when we see no apparent purpose. As long as we are the judge and jury to the type of suffering we endure and its length, then we do not hate the pain.

Divorce, mental illness, family tragedy, sexual abuse, loneliness, and death are some of life's most challenging potholes on the road to righteousness. These can happen out of nowhere – loss of a loved one, unexpected infidelity. When we are unclear about the purpose, we avoid pain at all costs. Yet all of it has purpose if we are willing to change our perspective.

In the passage above, the Bible starts with the word, "Therefore…" The starting blocks for this race are found in **Hebrews 11**. The Hebrew writer calls the reader to draw strength from former contenders in the faith. As we enter life's proverbial track meet, we see that our race is not the first. Several other incredible champions of faith have run before us.

Hebrews 11 lists some of them: Moses, Rahab, Sarah, and a list of other characters who were not perfect by any stretch of the imagination. Moses stuttered and murdered. Abraham lied. Rahab prostituted herself, David committed adultery,

Sarah a doubted. This is not a list of perfect people or even heroes. It is a list of sinners who put their trust in God and watched Him do amazing things. Their lives are an example for us.

In our fellowship of churches, we also have amazing examples of people who put their hope and trust in God through difficult situations. Blaise Feumba risked his life in the midst of a civil war in Africa to keep his family safe. He witnessed a militant army go as far as cutting babies out of pregnant women, then holding the baby up in the air. He has seen human life reduced to the most debased form of living on the face of the earth. Yet he is still preaching in Africa. He has overcome bitterness at the highest level.

Cassidy Olmos is another example to me. She suffered two miscarriages on the foreign mission field. Her beautiful smile and loyal heart make us forget this potential injury to her faith. Maria Hart stands next to her, having knowingly carried a son, named Wesley, full-term, only to see him die a few hours later. Ashley Tambaur overcame the betrayal of a husband who came out as gay after she married righteously in the Kingdom, to marry again and continue preaching. Michele Williamson overcame sexual abuse, racial abuse, emotional abuse, family incest, and narcissistic behavior. There are others like Michael and Sharon Kirchner, Nick and Denise Bordieri, Raul and Lynda Moreno, Tim and Lianne Kernan, the Untalans, Sullivans, Causeys, and Blackwells, alongside the Smellies and Beases. Each has their own unique story of rejecting bitterness to keep following Jesus.

God says that there is a race marked out for each of us. The Greek word for race is *agona*. It means struggle and is also where we get the word agony. Just like Jesus, we are encouraged to embrace the race and agony that is individual to us.

Jesus is said to have endured the cross, scorning its shame *"for the joy set before Him."* What was that joy? In other words, what was the purpose in the pain? The salvation of the world. Jesus knew His pain would fuel worldwide salvation. Therefore, He burned pain as fuel for the journey.

Burton Coffman's Bible commentary describes this joy in amazing technicolor:

> The joy that was set before him was the joy of reversing, at last, the tragic defeat of humanity in the Paradise of Eden; the joy of knowing that Satan's purpose of destroying man was foiled; the joy of "bringing many sons unto glory;" **(Hebrews 2:10)** the joy of the saved entering heaven "with songs of everlasting joy upon their heads;" **(Isaiah 35:10)** the joy of the herald angels' "tidings of great joy to all people;" **(Luke 2:10)** and such marvelous joy that, in truth, no vocabulary may describe it, no rhetoric suggest it, or finite mind fully conceive of it. Placed in the balances of consideration and weighed against the epic sufferings our Lord passed through, that unspeakable joy overwhelmingly prevailed. It was precisely this type of weighing one thing against another that Paul had in mind when he wrote the

Corinthians, *"For our light affliction, which is for the moment, worketh for us more and more exceedingly an eternal weight of glory."* **(2 Corinthians 4:17)**

The scripture also says to throw off the sin and distractions that entangle us in our race. The Hebrew writer argues that sins and distractions can hold us back. Sin is usually obvious, but distractions are not necessarily sin. Even good things can be a distraction and can hurt our race. The Greek word for entangle is *euperistaton* and means "easily admired." Some sins are easily avoided and some are easily admired. In the past I admired bitterness, and it distracted me from my journey until I saw its devastating impact on my life and the lives of others around me.

That is why the purity of our hearts is so necessary to see God through suffering. **(Matthew 5:9)** When we see God through our grief, we are "supremely blessed, and well off" – the meaning of the Greek word for blessed, or (*μακάριοι*). God's plan to prepare us for true joy is often packaged in pain. Joseph's preparation to lead all Israel was bundled in the painful abandonment by his brothers. David's ascent and preparation for the throne was clothed in 20 years of running as a fugitive. Jesus gift-wrapped Peter's preparation as a movement's leading evangelist in the pain of his sinful denial.

When we are at the peak of our pain and so frustrated we scream, "I hate this," we have stopped seeing any legitimate reason for the struggle. We need to remember the assurance Jesus gave Peter, *"I've prayed for you, and when you turn back, strengthen your brothers…"* **(Luke 22:32)** The pain of Peter's sin prepared him to deliver the inaugural address on forgiveness at Pentecost, strengthening over three thousand new brothers and sisters. He knew what it felt to be cut to the heart and forgiven. Our Lord understands that He has to do something to us before He can do something through us.

Words cannot express how grateful I am for my past. When I was abandoned, I wandered around like an empty shell, devoid of all feelings. I turned my bitterness on countless victims through immorality, deceit, and sensuality. After acknowledging the pain, the sadness I felt was indescribable. God was giving me a microscopic view of what He feels daily. It gave me a deep conviction on being loyal to God. The pain I caused God is still at the forefront of my mind. Indeed, His grace is still amazing!

Moreover, the education I received in suffering is invaluable. I learned that we do not have to be great to get started, but we have to get started to be great. Fear of failure cannot outweigh our desire to succeed. I have also learned that crisis can be a divine opportunity. The Chinese language recognizes this, using the same word for danger and opportunity.

The level of resilience and determination I now have is unquestionably a testament to surviving my past. I have learned that worry will never empty tomorrow of sorrow; instead, it empties today of its strength. Suffering also taught me that the bitterness of our past must die to let the power of our future begin. We suffer the pain of discipline or the pain of regret. We endure the pain of humility or the pain of humiliation.

The lessons I have learned from my suffering are priceless assets as an evangelist, and it brings me to tears of joy that God counted me worthy to suffer for His glory. My life is my message.

> *Consider it pure joy, my brothers and sisters, whenever you face trials of many kinds, because you know that the testing of your faith produces perseverance. Let perseverance finish its work so that you may be mature and complete, not lacking anything. If any of you lacks wisdom, you should ask God, who gives generously to all without finding fault, and it will be given to you. But when you ask, you must believe and not doubt, because the one who doubts is like a wave of the sea, blown and tossed by the wind. That person should not expect to receive anything from the Lord. Such a person is double-minded and unstable in all they do.* **(James 1:2-8)**

Tears of Laughter

"He will yet fill your mouth with laughter and your lips with shouts of joy." **(Job 8:21)**

Not only does gratitude produce tears of joy, but they tend to spin out into a never-ending carousel of laughter if you take the time to see the comedy in the chaos. Michele and I laugh, a lot. Most often, she teases me (affectionately), and I help her find the humor in the hardship or a comical message in the mess. Some evenings, we laugh so hard that we cry, wiping away tears like two children secretly sharing jokes in elementary school.

We each have our miniature alter egos – crazy character voices used when calling one another out. I could be teasing her for asking too many questions before 7am, like I'm in a tribunal, or she could be pretending that my leadership is like riding a motorcycle without a helmet at 120 miles per hour scared to death. It all culminates in laughter.

We've even developed a motto in our household: "Let the differences between you create fascination, not frustration."

My wife has always appreciated, or maybe at times just tolerated, my artsy side. It doesn't matter if it is my late Sunday night headphone personal disco, or my obsession with sports or the latest trend, she always supports me, even if with a bit of a smirk. The thing she likes best though is to laugh her head off going through my old modelling pictures. The melodramatic poses, the chin-jutting swagger sometimes masked insecurity and other times were me acting like I was the creator of confidence. She laughs at the cheeky squint that screams, "Get Calvin Klein on the phone now." Some of the shots show a man who's owning the camera, others are a mix of ambition and a lack of self-awareness. I'll watch her flip through them half proud, half playful disbelief. She'll scroll through personal shots alongside model pictures and smile in agreement until, out of nowhere – bang – there it is.

The legendary cross-eyed picture of me leading one of my first weddings!

It is a perfectly timed moment of leadership brilliance with eyes that look like they are trying to read two completely different verses of Scripture simultaneously. I denied it forever until I finally looked at the photo and confirmed, "I'm cross-eyed" in that shot. Both eyes were totally doing their own thing. I had to laugh at myself. This shot is a reminder that I can never take myself too seriously. This laughter is the special ingredient, a type of secret sauce in our marriage. It is a laughter that produces tears of its own.

When we sit down and look through old pictures, Michele looks for any photo where my eyes look like they are doing the "Cupid shuffle." It is a family tradition. She insists it is God's way of embarrassing my coolness.

In return, I lovingly tease her about her Asian heritage and its intense attention to detail. She is the type of person who is super-sensitive to everyone around her. I always joke about it, saying "Sweetie, there are 8 billion humans on the planet. Trust me … nobody's looking at you."

Here's the truth, though. We laugh because we've cried. We joke because we have survived. We banter because we discovered healing in each other.

When you have been through trauma, laughter is not just humor – it's therapy.

There are occasions when we go back to our exaggerated selves to mitigate a rebuke, to humanize an admission, or to diffuse the tension of a solemn discussion. It is our way of giving one another mercy, in the guise of humor. It works. One look, one voice, and an avalanche of laughter comes rushing out. The severity is lost, and the tears roll – not tears of grief, but of happiness.

We laugh at all of it. We laugh at my insecurity being in control of the house – like when she puts her hand on my shoulder as if taking command. I automatically change position like a linebacker re-establishing control. We laugh at her speaking in "ancient Egyptian hieroglyphics" and then getting upset that I cannot decipher her silence. We laugh at our mother or "Daddy" issues when they come up. We die laughing, playfully calling each other martyrs.

We both understand that a lot of our quirks, personalities, and eccentricities are a result of the trauma we have experienced. Rejection, abuse, abandonment – it has all shaped us in individual ways. But it did not conquer us. Now, instead of resentment, we prefer to banter. We use our stories to get close to one another, not to hide behind. We use our sense of humor as a sacred healing ground.

I am a lone, surviving black man "with a cat," writing a book called *Tears*. So much for the tough guy reputation.

Even through the tears, tension, and trauma, joy has become the byproduct of dealing with everything with God - a real joy, not callous or condescending. Laughter is a way of saying "Life's too heavy not to laugh sometimes." Sometimes, joy is all that is left for survival. The Bible says, *"A cheerful heart is good medicine, but a crushed spirit dries up the bones."* **(Proverbs 17:22)**

Science verifies this as well. Laughter releases endorphins, the body's natural mood boosters, and suppresses cortisol, the stress hormone. It stimulates immune function, lowers blood pressure, and increases pain tolerance. Most incredibly at all, research shows that laughter can trigger tears because the body is overcome with an emotion it just can't contain.

Laughter is how the soul exhales. Tears-of-joy laughter is proof your soul is still in touch with being human. It doesn't mean your hurt is funny, but it is usually a sign that it is finally behind you.

Joy doesn't mean your life is perfect. It means your soul is still dancing, even with a limp. Laughter is the sound of a soul that's been set free.

Chapter 8: Tears of Laughter and Joy

Conclusion

I've cried tears of brokenness, tears of truth, tears of darkness, and even tears of betrayal. Through it all, I've come to embrace what I once resisted: pain has a purpose. Jesus Christ learned obedience through what He suffered, and I've chosen to embody this passage as well. **(Hebrews 5)** Each tear has taught me something about myself, about others, and most of all, about God. The searing pain of loss, the crushing weight of betrayal, the deafening silence of suffering... what once seemed senseless now breathes with significance. It has all been woven into a greater fabric of lifelong faith.

> *And we know that in all things God works for the good of those who love Him, who have been called according to His purpose.* **(Romans 8:28)**

Nothing happens *to you* – everything happens *for you*. This perspective is exclusive to those who love God.

The tears I cry today are not from depression or despair – they are from depth. They no longer come from worry or weakness, but from wisdom born in the furnace of affliction. Jaded memories no longer drive my tears, but joyful expectation and Godly transformation now fill me with tears. I shed no tears from helplessness; all tears shed now are from healing. The challenges that wounded me through faith now work for me, so there are no tears from breakdown but breakthrough. I now carry a deep conviction: every injury is an invitation. An invitation to love, to rise, to become extraordinary – or to fade into obscurity. Pain hollowed out parts of my heart, but golden faith has filled in the cracks. Tears are not the end of the story; they are the valuable ink that writes the next chapter. As it's been said, you can be phenomenal or be forgotten. It was Christopher Wren who purposely chose a charred stone with a phoenix atop St Paul's Cathedral after the Great Fire of London. God has also given me the choice several times to rebuild from ashes. And you can too.

I've chosen to rise.

Tears have the power to transform an ice-cold heart into a tender soul. Through suffering, I've learned that I am what I choose to be. The secret to living is being a disciple who's giving. God often rewards the selfless the most on the day they feel like giving up. Perseverance always prevails when everything else fails. As my son in the faith, "Anthony Olmos," says, never give up, never give in, stay all in!

Suffering taught me to believe in myself because I had to speak life into myself when no one else did. I've learned that low self-talk leads to even lower self-belief. Suffering also taught me this: your life will either be an example or a warning. I've chosen to be an example by the grace of God. Yes, I've made terrible mistakes along the way. And yes, horrible things have been done to me. But I refuse to let those things define my destiny. There is no virtue in victimization, just emotional isolation that kills your motivation.

I am grateful. Gratitude has taught me to appreciate what I have, rather than constantly trying to have what I want. It has turned survival into strength, and strength into song.

Now, I invite you to join me on this journey. Cry if you must. Grieve what was. Feel it all. But don't stop there. Let every tear become a prayer, and a bridge to a beautiful sunrise. Let every wound become well. Let your tears carry you–not into defeat, but into destiny.

I did it at 14. I did it at 18. I did it at 25. And I'm still doing it. Because life isn't about finding yourself, a Godly life is about creating yourself.

As Charlie Chaplin once said, "A day without a smile is a day lost." So let your tears water the soil of joy. Let them fall like the walls of Jericho. And when the weeping is over… smile. Because the sun still rises. And so do we.

Conclusion

Printed in Great Britain
by Amazon